MAPPING SOCIAL GAZE

A Discourse on Culture and Democracy

MAPPING SOCIAL GAZE

A Discourse on Culture and Democracy

Editors
Badri Narayan • K.N. Bhatt

G.B. Pant Memorial Lectures Series
Part-I

Vani Book Company

Vani Book Company
Head Office

4695, 21-A, Daryaganj, New Delhi 110 002, India
Phone +91 11 23273167 Fax : +91 11 23275710

Registered Bookstores and Offices

Ashok Rajpath, Patna 800 004, Bihar
Coffee House Campus, Mahatma Gandhi Marg, Allahabad 211 001, Uttar Pradesh
Mahatma Gandhi International Hindi University, Wardha 442 001, Maharashtra
Sultania Road, Moti Park, Bhopal 462 001, Madhya Pradesh
Goripur Taliya Para, 313, R.B.C. Road 24- Parganas (North) Kolkata 743 166, West Bengal

www.vaniprakashan.in
marketing@vaniprakashan.in
sales@vaniprakashan.in

Mapping Social Gaze : A Discourse on Culture and Democracy
Edited by Badri Narayan, K.N. Bhatt

ISBN : 978-93-88434-98-0
Social Science

First Edition 2019

Price : ₹ 299

Printed and bound in India at City Press, Delhi-110 095

Vani Prakashan's signature motif is created by Artist Maqbool Fida Husain

Dedicated to Prof. S.C. Dubey, Prof. A.D. Pant,
Prof. S.P. Nagendra, Prof. Janak Pandey,
Prof. R.C. Tripathi for their visionary leadership.

Preface

The Govind Ballabh Pant Social Science Institute (GBPSSI), Allahabad has been organizing the G. B. Pant Memorial Lectures since 1980. Until 2019, thirty four lectures have been delivered by eminent social scientists and have attracted students and academics from the city of Allahabad in large numbers. Each lecture has been a testimonial of the contemporary times. The Institute has initiated a series of volumes, publishing these lectures. The readers would travel through the maze of time and see how Indian economy, politics and society unfold in the last four decades.

In September 2014 soon after the General Elections to the Indian Parliament when the Bhartiya Janta Party swept almost all constituencies in Uttar Pradesh, Chhattisgarh, Madhya Pradesh, Rajasthan and also Bihar, Shaibal Gupta delivered the 29th Govind Ballabh Pant Memorial Lecture, 'Idea of the Hindi Heartland', at the Govind Ballabh Pant Social Science Institute, Allahabad. He attempted to answer the question as to why the tectonic shift in national ruling political configuration (in 2014) is being considered as a capture by the Hindi heartland. Shaibal drew upon historical and literary sources to establish an identity of the Hindi heartland, which he described as a dynamic interplay of gender, religion and politics in the region with its multiplicities, plurality and uncertainties.

A year earlier, in September 2013, delivering the 28th Memorial Lecture, 'Constitutional Morality and the Administration of Justice', Kalpana Kannabiran discussed the potential for subaltern interpretation of constitutional morality by communities that faced historical injustice and explored possibilities of a vision that drives movements for social transformation. She viewed constitutional morality as an intrinsic part of larger project of morality in politics that nourished a free ranging intellectual life and democratic possibility rooted in democratic political struggle. Kalpana hoped that an easy recourse to public morality and a truncated reading of the constitution by the courts, especially Article 15, would be resisted by the other within and outside courts in a manner that a social and economic revolution would gradually take place while preserving the freedom and dignity of the individual.

The third memorial lecture, 'Culture in Contact : Acculturation and Change', by John W. Berry was scripted in 1997. He elaborated on the then very largely accepted fact that all contemporary societies are culturally plural and its diversities are reflected in national societies and institutions. And this plurality is embraced in all groups, sedentary or migrants, refugees and indigenous peoples, and also by institutions formal or informal. Berry spoke in 1997. Since then India has seen redefinition of cultural pluralism, rights of refugees, migrants and the tribals, and also the role of institutions.

And the first two Lectures were scripted some five years ago. Five years is not considered a long period in a nation's history. Perhaps, it is not so. Reading these would tell a discerning reader how circumstances have changed in the last few years as India approaches 2020 with a new social order.

–Pradeep Bhargava
Department of Economics
Indira Gandhi National Tribal University
Place : Amarkantka
Date : 10 August, 2019

Introduction

G.B. Pant Social Science Institute, Jhusi, Prayagraj has a tradition of organizing G.B. Pant Memorial lectures on the occasion of foundation day of Institute. Under the lecture series, the eminent scholars deliver this prestigious lecture around their area of expertise. The lecture series focusses on issues important in the contemporary social science discourses. This lecture series was started in the year 1980 when the institute was founded. Since then it is continuously being organized on the occasion of our foundation day. The scholars such as P.N. Haksar, P.C. Joshi, V.K.R.V. Rao, Y.K. Alagh, Ramkrishna Mukherjee, A.R. Desai, M.S. Gore, G.C. Pandey, Ravindra Kumar, S.C. Dube, John W. Berry, D.N. Dhanagre, Amiya K. Baghchi, Jean Dreze, Sudipta Kaviraj, Montek Singh Ahluwalia, Swapna Das Gupta, Ramachandra Guha and many more has delivered this lecture so far.

G.B. Pant Social Science Institute, a constituent institute of Central University Allahabad, is a premiere research and development institute in India. The Institute is unique in its concerns with both theoretical and applied research in social and management sciences, particularly in the fields of socio-economic development, popular culture, public policies and social technologies of modernity. The main areas of research at the Institute include development planning and policy, environment, population and health, human development, rural development and management, culture, power and change, democracy and institutions. Interdisciplinary perspectives in social research, development and management are encouraged with a keen commitment to build up a comprehensive and integrated approach to various developmental, educational and cultural aspects of nation building. As part of its diversification and specialization of functions, the Institute undertakes studies and research on various aspects of socio-economic change and development of Indian states. These themes and socio-academic concerns of the institute also reflects on the topic of the G.B. Pant memorial lectures selected by scholars every years.

G.B. Pant Social Science Institute, Prayag Raj has a plan to publish these lectures in a series of volumes evolved around various themes. The Vani Prakashan Delhi under the series of Vani Book Company has kindly agreed to bring out this series of publication in collaboration with GBPSSI. The first volume named 'Mapping Social Gaze : A Discourse on Culture and Democracy' is ready here for the readers. This volume contains three lectures delivered by

Kalpana Kannabiran, Shaibal Gupta and John W. Berry. These three lectures deal with deeper aspects of culture and Making of democracy.

Kalpana Kannabiran in her lecture 'Constitutional Morality & the Imagination of Justice', has tried to answer that "what are the possible contours of a transformative constitutionalism?" Here, she doesn't talk about the constitutional law but the vision that drives movements for Social Transformation, & provides a framework for radical struggle on different fronts.

While being in the possible articulations of constitutional morality, she has delineated the connection between liberty, non- discrimination and pluralism as the heart of this work. The interconnections between Article 14 & Article 21 are immediate & inextricable. This is a good attempt to dismantle disciplinary protocols and use a range of materials to understand the problem

Shaibal Gupta in his lecture 'Idea of the Hindi Heartland' has tried to answer numerous questions regarding the tangibility or the speculative realm of Hindi Heartland. Is it geographical expression only or also a coherent cultural construct? Is it a contemptuous specification or otherwise? Why Hindi Heartland has suddenly come to the centre stage? And many more.

To answer all these questions, he started by connecting it with the eve of independence, how union government decided Hindi Heartland as an electoral field. Then he turns the discussion towards the geographical importance of it. Meanwhile, he has said that it's generally a conservative idea in India.

He carries forward his discussion of Hindi Heartland in different dimensions. Some of them are- Mystique Triad of Brahmins, Benaras & Banias, Identity issue in Hindi Heartland and Development Experience in Hindi Heartland. He concludes that the idea of Hindi Heartland is self explanatory.

John W. Berry in his lecture on 'Cultures in Contact : Acculturation and Change' has categorized the whole discussion in different dimensions around the issues such as multiculturalism, Immigration and the Changing Population profile, Ethnic and Race Relations, Immigrant Acculturation, Social Benefits and Costs of Multiculturalism Policy. Implications for Immigration & multiculturalism Policy. His discourse here is based on his study and experience of Canadian Society.

Berry starts with a brief introduction of his paper, followed by a set of ideas, some empirical findings and a few practical implications for living together in plural settings. He further describes that there are many reasons for a society to become culturally plural. He has explained his discourses with clearly enumerated diagrams.

Institute is thankful to Vani Prakashan Group for agreeing to publish these volumes. We also express our gratitude to the contributors of this volume who supported this idea. These lectures were firstly printed and published as separate lecture by the institute and now appearing in this volume. We hope this volume will help academicians, researcher and students to capture the social gaze.

Content

Constitutional Morality and the Imagination of Justice

Kalpana Kannabiran

Introduction

This project has been driven by a question. What are the possible contours of a transformative constitutionalism? In the framing of this question, the constitution is not constitutional law, it is not confined to constitutional courts, nor is it accessible for judicial interpretation alone. It is a vision that drives movements for social transformation, and provides a framework for radical struggle on different fronts. It is the autochthonous framework within which a diligent administration, judiciary or legislature might locate it self. It contains the potential for the subaltern interpretation of constitutional morality by communities that face historical injustice and their advocates.

Within the range of possible articulations of constitutional morality, the connection between liberty, non-discrimination and pluralism at the heart of this work. To understand the different layers of this connection, I have used Article 15 of the Constitution of India as my point of departure, examining its scope and problematising established interpretations of its reach. The interconnections between Article 15 and Article 21, between discrimination and the curtailment/negation/loss of liberty are immediate and in extricable. In opening this field out therefore, it is important to move

'Constitutional Morality and the Imagination of Justice', 1oth September, 2013
G.B. Pant Social Science Institute

beyond the traditional reading of equality with life, to look instead at the possibilities of reading non-discrimination with liberty. This move can be accomplished effectively with the use of a differently constructed corpus of materials that enable a different reading. And this is the second part of what I have attempted to do to dismantle disciplinary protocols and use a range of materials to understand the problem of discrimination in the law. Methodologically, this would mean (redeploying Guha with a twist) comprehending apparently unanticipated arguments by means of analogy, "by an awareness and understanding of a relation between forms. Just as one learns the use of a new language by freeing one's way from the known elements to the unknown, comparing and contrasting unfamiliar sounds and meanings with familiar ones" (Guha 1983, 2), so also may we revisit constitutional categories and discourse, to map presences and absences, interrogate established usages and propose new ones that draw from the old by affirmation, extension,negation, comparison or analogy.

This paper has two sections. In the first section, I will attempt today to set out some signposts which might be productive for a different imagination of justice and then in the second section I move on to examine the field of constitutional morality, focusing especially on the relationship between non-discrimination and liberty with reference to six indices disability, caste, tribe, religion, and gender women and sexual minorities as symbols of gender marginality.

Section I : General Framework

Situating Constitutional Morality

At every moment of social upheaval, public debate is torn as under by the tension between different moral orders and competing moral claims. This is especially the case when sexual assault/sexual violence is at the centre of the debate in India. Without going in to the details of articulations that are all too familiar, I will take off from constitutional conversations. 'Constitutional morality' is a term developed during the era of constitution making in the 1940s by the Indian philosopher and architect of the Indian Constitution, B. R. Ambedkar, specifically in the context of aggravated and violent discrimination against the castes situated at the bottom of the Hindu social order. Simply stated it recognises that the constitutional order may not represent a "natural" sentiment but must never the less be cultivated by people, even when it directly contradicts their personal beliefs, when such beliefs and practices perpetrate injustice and oppression on classes at the bottom of the social order. The sketch of constitutional morality provided by Ambedkar addresses the insurgent imperative in the constitution, and erodes in fundamental ways the encrustation of the norm of discrimination in the body politic (Ambedkar [1948] 2002, 484). Constitutional morality then, is an intrinsic part of a larger project of morality in politics that nourishes a free ranging intellectual life and democratic political possibility rooted in democratic political struggle.

It is pertinent here to draw a distinction between the constitutional vision drawn out by Ambedkar and constitutional law deliberated on in courts of different jurisdictions in India. Brown argues that while both moralism and morality might constitute their identity by distancing themselves from power, they are not equivalents (Brown 2001, 22). This may be extended to an understanding of the contrast between the moralism of constitutional interpretation (constitutional law) and the Ambedkarite formulation of constitutional morality. Constitutional jurisprudence on non-discrimination provides for us an immediate demonstration of the fact that morality "persistently risk(s) devolving into moralism" (Brown 2001, 22), which is "an impoverished substitute for, or reaction to, the evisceration of a sustaining moral vision" (Brown 2001, 23) and "tends to be intensely antagonistic toward a richly agonistic political or intellectual life" (Brown 2001, 30).

In its classic form, I would argue, constitutional jurisprudence depoliticizes the reading of non-discrimination, by decontextualising the political phenomenon of writing the constitution from comprehension of its historical emergence and from a recognition of the powers that produce and contour it" (Brown 2006, 15). This eschewing of power and history in the representation of its subject, results in the representation itself providing a truncated "ontological naturalness or essentialism" that then goes on to inform the entire field of constitutional jurisprudence.

The return to history and politics in constitutional hermeneutics can be accomplished effectively with the use of a differently constructed corpus of materials that enable a different reading. Methodologically, this would mean (redeploying Guha with a twist) comprehending apparently unanticipated arguments by means of analogy, by an 'awareness and understanding of a relation between forms'. Just as one learns the use of a new language by feeling one's way from the known elements to the unknown, comparing and contrasting unfamiliar sounds and meanings with familiar ones' (Guha 1983, 2), so also may we revisit constitutional categories and discourse, to map presences and absences, interrogate established usages and propose new ones that draw from the old by affirmation, extension, negation, comparison or analogy.

Liberty and Discrimination

If justice is freedom, or more specifically liberty, then, as Bauman argues, "freedom is itself a social fact, socially produced and socially endowed with the meaning it happens to carry at a particular time or place" (Bauman [1988] 1997, 28). Drawing on Norbert Elias, Bauman uses "sociogenesis of freedom" to refer to "those departures and dislocations in social figurations, large and small, which led to successive modifications in the network of dependencies and hence also in the contexts of human interaction, and which the discourse of freedom articulated. It is assumed that every such dislocation created social tensions appearing to contemporaries as an unresolved social problem, either demanding the rejection of past concepts or their innovative use" (Bauman [1988] 1997, 30). In order to map the evolution of a sociogenesis of liberty, so to speak, at this historical moment, we need then to "articulate experiences of new social structures and processes, to render the change meaningful" (Bauman [1988] 1997, 29).

Taking a different route, Rawls delineates two principles of justice, where the full enjoyment of the most extensive scheme of equal basic liberties is the precondition for the distribution of wealth and income (Rawls 1999 [1971]: 53). "[I]nfringement of the basic equal liberties protected by the first principle, cannot be justified, or compensated for, by greater social and economic advantages" (Rawls

1999 [1971] : 53- 54), nor can there be any "exchanges between basic liberties and economic and social gains except under extenuating circumstances" (Rawls 1999 [1971]: 55). Inequalities, by this token, are permissible [and fair, or just] only in so far as they are to everyone's advantage and more importantly, come into play after the guarantee of liberty is accomplished. Sen interrogates Rawls' "downplaying" of the possibility that different people "can have widely varying opportunities to convert general resources (like income and wealth) into capabilities what they can or cannot actually do...[which] reflect pervasive variations... in the human condition and in the relevant social circumstances" (Sen 2009 : 261). This obstruction that people face in converting resources into opportunities that are embedded in social circumstances is discrimination, not just inequality.

In a manner of speaking, we are here entering the debate on two sets of rights social and economic rights and civil and political rights. Supiot, in asserting the centrality of social and economic rights, argues for instance that people concern themselves with the defence of freedoms only when minimum physical and economic security is assured : "freedom is impossible where physical or economic insecurity prevail" (Supiot 2007 : 199). Yet, physical insecurity itself is the loss of freedom the loss of liberty, as I hope to demonstrate through the discussion on gender that follows. And if economic insecurity engenders dependence, is insecurity economic and physical itself not the loss of liberty?

When may we consider that the guarantee of liberty has been established? Challenging the liberal understanding of freedom that force or the coercive threat of it constitute the only forms of constraint that interfere with individual liberty, Skinner invokes the insistence of neo-roman writers that "to live in a condition of dependence is in itself a source and a form of constraint As soon as you recognise that you are living in such a condition, this will serve in itself to constrain you from exercising a number of your civil rights...[T]o live in such a condition is to suffer a diminution not merely of security for your liberty but of liberty itself" (Skinner 1998:84). The anticipation (or danger) of coercion erodes liberty, by this argument.

It is not out of place in speaking about liberty, to recall Bauman's analysis of Bentham's panopticon, as a model of a mini society [which echoes Ambedkar's observations on the republic of the Touchables] precisely because it details for us the specific ways in which discrimination restrains liberty :

"Some actors are freer than others : discrimination in the degree of freedom allotted to various categories of actors is the very stuff of which the social system is moulded. Discrimination precedes action...Instead of being an unanticipated outcome of the interplay between "phenomenologically equal", similarly free agents, social order is something which some people set for others...If it is true that "men make society", it is also true that some men make the kind of society in which other men must live and act. Some people set norms, some other people follow them" (Bauman [1988], 1997, 23).

Is liberty the Siamese twin of non-discrimination? Important to this exercise is the specificity of the condition of liberty to the grounds of discrimination. To anticipate my argument, while non-discrimination might be a shared trope, liberty presents clearly distinct faces in relation to caste, sex, religion, tribe, disability, etc. And even where the question of liberty figures quite evidently in non-discrimination claims the connection is never established because of the disaggregative norm of interpretation that bases itself on the constitutional fragment "on grounds only of sex, caste, language, place of birth or any of them" (Article 15, emphasis added).

Hostile Environments

The concept of hostile environments is relevant especially to an understanding of the complex interconnections between discrimination and the curtailment of liberty.

The initial application of the concept of hostile environments has been to closed or (bounded) environments classrooms and closed learning spaces like campuses; work places that are spatially bounded; generally spaces where the person engaging in intimidating conduct is in close, daily proximity and interaction with the person being intimidated. The guidelines issued by the Supreme Court in Vishakha reflect this as well. However, the legal history of sexual harassment at the workplace in India has a specificity that bears reiteration. In the first case that came up before the Supreme Court, which, I believe laid the ground for Vishakha, Rupan Bajaj, while it was undoubtedly workplace harassment, it was an official social gathering outside a work setting not a bounded workplace. And yet, Bajaj was obstructed at every stage from seeking legal redress in a case that was one of public sexual humiliation. When she did secure justice, one media report observed, "It some how makes the law of the land look grotesquely odd and incongruous that a man who has done signal service to the country by ridding a state of the dread and oppression of terrorism should have to spend five months in jail for a minute's exuberance provoked by the charms of an attractive working woman". The lead article in another newspaper was more censorious of women: And women are expected to use "finely tuned, discreet social mechanisms for coping with importunate intrusions on the individual body".

These media reports take us to the core of the idea of hostile environments being an indispensable tool of discrimination. By curtailing liberty, hostile environments entrench discrimination and guarantee impunity to all expressions of public morality ranging from derogatory speech and expression to collective violence.

The pre-history of Vishakha complicates this situation some what more. The petitioners in Vishakha, a women's group went to court seeking protections for women at the workplace, after Bhanwari Devi had been sexually assaulted by dominant caste landlords because of her work in the government campaign against child marriage in Rajasthan. The workplace in Bhanwari's case was the village where she lived and worked. It was not a closed bounded space. What she was subjected to was not harassment but sexual assault. The hostility was generated, not only because she was a woman but because she was a dalit woman, nor was it confined to her village alone, because the hostility spread along lines of caste dominance and permeated village, administrative and judicial spaces. Ironically, while we have the Vishakha guidelines in place, and sexual harassment has been recognized as a form of gender based discrimination in the workplace, Bhanwari has not secured redress.

Discourses around 'honour,' 'shame' and 'modesty' draw their logic from hostile environments that fetter the minds and bodies of women in intractable ways, often prompting women to suspend their liberty in an attempt to make peace with environments that engender hostility.

How may we expand the idea of hostile environments to speak to the convergence of discrimination with the loss of liberty across the field not limiting it to gender based discrimination alone?

Section II : Reading Constitutional Morality

It is productive to begin by examining the definition of discrimination in the Indian Constitution :

15. (1) The State shall not discriminate against any citizen on grounds only of religion, race, caste, sex, place of birth or any of them.

(2) No citizen shall, on grounds only of religion, race, caste, sex, place of birth or any of them, be subject to any disability, liability, restriction or condition with regard to :

(a) access to shops, public restaurants, hotels and places of public entertainment; or

(b) the use of wells, tanks, bathing ghats, roads and places of public resort maintained wholly or partly out of State funds or dedicated to the use of the general public.

The first clause speaks to the vertical application of the right to non- discrimination, between the state and the citizen; the second clause speaks to the horizontal application of the right, between citizens inter se. Picking up the thread of Article 15(2) is Article 17, which bans the practice of untouchability in any form a provision that is aimed at disciplining the state and citizen, both. The key to the meaning of the phrase "shall not discriminate" in 15(1), is contained in 15(2) subjecting a person to any disability, liability, restriction or condition [implicitly detrimental] on grounds of religion, race, caste, sex, place of birth or any of them would amount to discrimination. The idea of liberty is invoked in investing "discrimination" with meaning the substance of 15(2) is that no citizen's freedom may be curtailed on the specified grounds. Moving further down to 15(3), 15(4) and 15(5), because discrimination is a curtailing conduct that operates indirectly as well as directly, the remedy also necessitates the creation of special provisions to combat discrimination. In this framework, the use of the terms "protective discrimination" and "compensatory discrimination" in jurisprudence and constitutional analysis to describe these provisions needs to be problematised as contradictions in terms that create the discursive possibility for equivocation on the important question of reservation. More recent legislation, notably the proposed amendment to the Persons with Disabilities Act adopts the definition of discrimination from the United Nations Convention on the Protection of Rights of Persons with Disabilities (UNCRPD), which like the Convention on the Elimination of all forms of Discrimination against Women (CEDAW) provides a broad based inclusive definition of discrimination as : "...any distinction, exclusion or restriction…which has the effect or purpose of impairing or nullifying the recognition, enjoyment or exercise ...on a basis of equality …of human rights and fundamental freedoms in the political, economic, social, cultural, civil or any other field." A quick comparison will demonstrate that the combined reading of 15(1) and 15(2) of the Constitution of India quoted above produces the same result.

The question of liberty will be examined at greater length as we move ahead.

Disability, as the first signpost in the analysis of discrimination, already overruns the interpretive boundaries of constitutional jurisprudence on Article 15. In looking at the constitutionally inarticulate index of disability, my attempt has been two-fold (at least): to interrogate the assumptions of able-normativity that wash over the entire range of ability based diversities and claims to non- discrimination; and to explore the specific position of persons with intellectual disabilities, who are constitutionally denied of equal citizenship, and whose "normal" habitation is a custodial facility.

However, disability rights discourse in and outside courts has tended not to engage with the politics of citizenship. While Butler addresses the problem of statelessness in relation to minorities expelled from the state or held in perpetuity in a condition of statelessness (Butler, Spivak 2007), this analysis of statelessness and sovereignty could be extended to politicize the right to non-discrimination of persons with disabilities.

Further, where disability is concerned, discrimination interlocks with the loss of liberty in two distinct ways: for the physically challenged, the routine denial of barrier free access perpetuates a hostile environment that physically and materially obstructs mobility the fact of requiring barrier free access translating by definition into lower levels of efficiency that require "accommodation" on the part of employers and institutions and "incentives" for compliance. For the intellectually challenged and the mentally ill, the problem of discrimination intersects with the loss of liberty through the denial of fundamental political rights and the legality of indefinite incarceration. For women with intellectual disability, it leads additionally to the increased vulnerability to sexual assault and the divesting by the state of any control over sexual/reproductive choice.

What is the relationship between consent and custody in the case of persons with disabilities? What are the limits of the state's contractarian approach to care for the profoundly disabled?

Disability does not find explicit mention in the guarantee of non discrimination in the Constitution of India. Article 15 reads, "The State shall not discriminate against any citizen on grounds only of religion, race, caste, sex, place of birth or any of them." Rather than allow this constitutional silence to rupture our reading of constitutional morality, it is more productive to attempt to write disability into the constitutional scheme through a radical interpretation of the constitution. Stepping aside from a minimalist approach that restricts disability to the purview of Article 14 alone, the decision of the Delhi High Court in Naz Foundation[1] gives us the methodological and interpretive tools to examine the substantive correspondence between Article 15 and the situation of persons with disabilities as is evident from state policy.

Article 15(2) recognizes the indispensability of barrier free access (liberty) to non-discrimination. This along with Article 17 that addresses the problem of segregation and exclusion and Article 21 that affirms the expansive right of every person to liberty[2] allows us to weave a tapestry of non-discrimination on grounds of disability out of constitutional threads.

Challenging the dominant view that it is only Articles 14 and 16 that are open to the ground of disability, we might return finally, to the use of analogous grounds in the Naz Foundation decision[3] and explore the possibility of constructing disability as a ground of discrimination analogous to sex and caste within the purview of Article 15[4]. These two indices are specifically relevant because of the overlap in discursive and social constructs between caste, sex and disability, an overlap that is far from irrelevant. Sex based discrimination echoes the arguments of frailty, reduced ability, incapacity of women in comparison with men arguments similar to the presumption of weakness, infirmity, incapacity and dependence of persons with disabilities. Official discourse on caste over the entire period stretching from the pre- constitutional to contemporary times appropriates the term "disability" to describe discrimination based on caste discrimination that manifests itself through segregation, exclusion and the denial of voice and visibility all of which, as I have illustrated, are themes that play out in specific ways with respect to disability.

Disability has provided the framework for the understanding of self- determination and social ability generally even in the context of the freedom struggle and the making of the Constitution – but remained invisible and inarticulate because it was [and continues to be] foundational. While "disability" serves as a point of reference for classes facing exclusion and discrimination, it has not been invoked self referentially to give voice and visibility to people with disabilities.

Caste is an issue that has attracted the widest range of scholars in law and sociology. I have attempted to compile a sociological corpus on caste drawing on the logic of the constitution, foregrounding in the process the intellectual history of non-discrimination based on caste, which must serve as a reference point for constitutional jurisprudence. There are insurmountable problems that arise from relying on materials that assume the normativity of the "upper caste" experience in deciding cases on the rights of the excluded castes, which I have attempted to demonstrate through a textual analysis of cases on reservation for the scheduled castes and scheduled tribes. In caste- based discrimination as well, we see a clear intersection between discrimination and liberty through the medium of Article 17 of the Constitution of India.

Untouchability is the form that the loss of liberty takes in a context of caste-based discrimination. This loss of liberty then quickly travels the road from untouchability to collective violence.

The massacres of dalits at Tsundur, Melavalavu and Khairlanji are attempts to police castes into subjugation and into acquiescence with a discriminatory social order. These were not spontaneous dominant caste bursts of anger and rage at the sight of the "untouchable" castes outside the prisons of untouchable locales. They were the culmination of an "open conspiracy" to stamp down any assertion of the right to liberty and the right to non-discrimination. In this and in cases of collective violence against minorities more generally, the traditional criminal jurisprudence on conspiracy needs to be revisited. The expression of conspiracy in structural violence is open and part of public morality – the "criminal meeting of minds ... writ large on the evidence brought on record," evidence that is neither circumstantial nor secretive. According to the Memorandum filed by the families of victims in the High Court of Andhra Pradesh in the Tsundur case, for instance.

"The fact that persons from four villages gathered at one time and place, that they were armed with deadly weapons, that they moved in unison according to a self-evident plan to attack the Scheduled Caste people," points to the commission of an offence under Section 149 of the Indian Penal Code, a section that was not applied by the trial court, even though there were convictions for eight murders and other acts of violence.[5]

There is need therefore to draw out the broad contours of constitutional morality and the informing interpretive strategies that might help craft an effective resistance to public morality through and outside courts of all jurisdictions.

The second and more "everyday expression" of the problem of liberty untouchability – is examined in the context of governmental action on untouchability (the S.R. Sankaran government orders) – in the mid 1970s in Andhra Pradesh also situating "the law" differently, and speaking to the need to engage with plural sites of law and justice, not limiting interventions to courts. Having said that, with three articles in the fundamental rights chapter of the Constitution speaking to the problem of untouchability, segregation and forced labour (which includes, importantly agrestic slavery and "manual scavenging"), recovering a sociology and social history of untouchability as well the resistance to it becomes urgent.

This history of constitutional categories is indispensable to the development of a jurisprudence of non-discrimination by courts Article 15(1) and 15(2) setting out the context for Article 15(3) and

15(4) with Article 17 unequivocally reinforcing the guarantee of non- discrimination through a proscription of its most extreme form. In appreciating this history, courts need to draw on subaltern social science that gives meaning to these categories and recovers the histories that necessitated the formulation of the categories in the first place.

The history of the dispossession of adivasis is a long and tortured one. However, while official discourse focuses on "backwardness" and exploitation by non-tribals, the language of discrimination is strangely not as explicit as it might be. Social movements on the other hand have identified discrimination by the state directly and through the concerted denial of due diligence as the experience of the range of adivasi communities. The problem of liberty here, is expressed through the ousting from land, through confinement in settlements, or through the tacit support to "settler populations" that dispossess adivasis on a day-to-day level. The continuity between the forest bureaucracies during colonialism and after has created a crisis of the curtailment of liberty and a seamlessness in practices of discrimination, segregation, stigmatization and exclusion. Here too, as in the case of caste, the convergence between diligent administrators and communities of resistance is critical.

The inclusion of "tribe" within the purview of Article 15(1) especially invites careful examination. The Constitution recognizes the need for special protections for scheduled castes and scheduled tribes, in all matters ranging from education to political participation. Interestingly, the category of "tribe" is not explicitly stated in Article 15(1), but it is defined in Article 366(25) in a circular manner : "Scheduled Tribes" means such tribes or tribal communities or parts of or groups within such tribes or tribal communities as are deemed under Article 342 to be Scheduled Tribes for the Purpose of the Constitution."

Paradoxically, while debates in the constituent assembly focused on the aboriginal tribes as being the original inhabitants (evident in Jaipal Singh's opening statement in the Constituent Assembly), there is no debate, on the omission of "tribe" from Article 15(1), nor later any explanation in constitutional jurisprudence for bringing "tribe" within the purview of Article 15(1) despite the inarticulation.

Article 15 (1) The State shall not discriminate against any citizen on grounds only of religion, race, caste, sex, place of birth or any of them."

It is my suggestion that protections for scheduled tribes against discrimination under Article 15 are contained in the explicit protections against discrimination based on "race" and "place of birth." The constitutional identification of the adivasi in India draws from the twin tracks of colonial anthropology and colonial administration and is simultaneously a racial and territorial identification. While the history is an embattled one, the intersectional interpretation of both non-discrimination (race) and liberty (place of birth) converges for this group alone in a single clause inArticle 15.

The racial and territorial identification of the category of "tribe" encapsulates the convergence of discrimination and loss of liberty as the historical experience of adivasi communities safeguards in relation to racial discrimination and territorial protections being inextricably linked. The territorial identification of tribes takes two constitutional forms areas that fall under Schedule V of the constitution, and areas that fall under Schedule VI. While these are both related in terms of the imagining of autonomy and self governance, there are structural differences in state formation that are rooted in the dispersal of adivasi communities across different states that were designated as Partially Excluded Areas (Schedule V) and the states of north east India that were designated as Excluded Areas (Schedule VI) under the Government of India Act, 1935. The derogation of the right to personal liberty in these two areas takes clearly distinct forms, with dispossession through displacement and non tribal enclavement being characteristic of the experience of Schedule V areas and dispossession through militarization and the indefinite use of the Armed Forces Special Powers Act being the experience of the Schedule VI areas. Neither forced displacement nor indefinite military occupation can be disconnected from the problem of discrimination against adivasi regions by the state because it can scarcely be forgotten that these are regions that are protected under the constitution.

To return to the problem of the strict application of 15(1), which is the approach courts have used especially in putting "disability" out of the purview of 15(1), the circular manner in which "tribe" is brought in without a specific mention, strengthens the case for the inclusion of disability, and bolsters the argument of analogous discrimination infinitely.

Wide ranging research has shown the diversity among Muslims in India, and also the overlaps between stratification systems among Muslims and the Hindu caste order (this is also the case with Christians, but this project focuses on the Muslim experience). The painstaking documentation of diversity among Muslims and the writing of the fact of diversity into the official record through the purposive transfer of social science research into legislative and judicial deliberations is accomplished by a radically constitutional administration, in the case of Andhra Pradesh represented by P.S. Krishnan.

Despite the existence of this diversity, evident also in the reservation for Muslim backward classes in different states, hindu majoritarianism homogenizes entire minorities through reductionist discourses of conversion, and prepares the ground for genocidal massacre on unprecedented scale. Collective violence then, is the form that the derogation of liberty takes with reference to religious minorities. But specific cases also demonstrate that a majoritarian jurisprudence can result discrimination and the derogation of liberty for women of minority communities the court then may in an inversion, become the site of violation, a possibility that must be eliminated.

To move now to gender, the observation of the majority in Madhu Kishwar v State of Bihar, that "[r]ules of succession are indeed susceptible of providing differential treatment, not necessarily equal. Non-uniformities would not in all events violate Article 14"[6] takes us to the heart of the matter. Does differential treatment and non-uniformity in the matter of succession constitute discrimination or does it not? What we witness here is an appropriation of the "special provisions" standard and its application against itself to justify discrimination.

In an attempt to resurrect a sense of justice, I have returned to the problem of an intellectual history of non-discrimination. Given the majoritarian slant in judicial discourse, especially evident in the re- iteration of hindu scriptures and the exposition of Manu-based worldviews in constitutional matters concerning women, the first step in treading a different path is to bring in the history of the early resistance to these worldviews. This would radically change the reference point of "tradition" and give women breathing space outside the scriptures. Since discrimination against women is most evident in the habit of violence, this project has attempted to map the habitations of violence before moving to an extensive analysis of case law on non- discrimination. Where women are concerned the derogation of liberty takes the form of sexual assault incarcerating women through sexual control and sexual violence.

The final part of the section on gender and indeed the entire project focuses on sexual orientation and sexual minorities. The extension of sex discrimination to a field that is not contained in the binary of male and female suddenly renders gender into a hyper-articulate index of discrimination. The history of contestation of binary categories of sex on the Indian sub-continent is a long and rich one that has been overlaid by the homogenizing force of Section 377 of the Indian Penal Code from the mid 1800s. Recovering that history enables a more layered understanding of the constitutional category of sex that has not been defined in Article 366 of the Constitution, and remains as such open to reinterpretation and revalorization. In an attempt to do this, I have looked at historiographies of sexuality in India which challenge the argument that the right of sexual minorities to non-discrimination is one that is rooted in the experience of the west and depart from the binary interpretation of sex as male or female, that has been adopted as the norm in constitutional law before Naz. This is not to suggest that the heteronorm is entirely imposed from without or that it gets completely dislodged by the heterogenous history of the politics of sexualities in contemporary India. Rather, the 'internal split of cultural difference within the same culture' (Spivak 2002 cf Bose and Bhattacharyya 2007, xxiv), opens out the view to "glaring discrepancies in the ways in which ethics play out across class and/ or power structures on the subcontinent", locating for us, critical moments of subalternity, which challenge the universal heterosexual norm within the same culture : "the entire fabric is not merely constituted of warp and weft but also of rip and tear and missing thread" (Bose and Bhattacharyya, xxv).

Zwilling and Sweet suggest that a "three-sex model was an important feature of the ancient Indian world view", drawing on brahmanical, Jain and Buddhist texts (Zwilling and Sweet 2000, 100).

While there was a negative value attached to the napumsaka, that state was not seen as an abnormality – Susruta and Caraka seeing the napumsaka as a true third sex with a biological origin and Jaina texts drawing a distinction between three sexes in terms of the numbers of muscles, veins and rice grains the mouth could hold (Zwilling and Sweet 2000, 110-111). Nor did any of these treatises speak of preventing the birth or conception of a napumsaka.

The Jaina delineation of sexes is more nuanced, also possibly counter brahmanical, in its re-valorization of veda to denote sexuality, in place of linga (113). Most importantly, "[b]y the fifth century CE, the Jains had severed the connection between the biological characteristics (dravyalinga) of sexuality and its psychological characteristics (bhavalinga) thus theoretically enabling a person of any biological sex to experience any of the three sexualities" (116). While such persons could not attain extra sensory knowledge, they could be perfected souls (119).

Against this historical backdrop, although we have had a radical advance in the Naz Foundation decision,[7] the problem of liberty even in the context of sexual minorities is far from resolved as the law restraining eunuchs shows. On the other side, the new proposed law that seeks to protect persons with disabilities from discrimination includes transgender communities within the category of "disorders in sexual development," taking the articulation of the right to non discrimination two steps back in a single sweep – medicalising the definition of disability within the deeply problematic framework of disorders, extending the reach from mental to sexual disorders; and falling back on the binary construction of sex/gender that the Naz Foundation decision dismantles so effectively.

Each of the indices of discrimination examined here have been the subject of international conventions, the movements against discrimination in the country engaging in deliberations at the national and international levels to sharpen the focus on such discrimination. The UN Convention on the Rights of Persons with Disabilities, the Convention on the Elimination of Racial Discrimination, the Rome Statute of the International Criminal Court, the UN Declaration on the Rights of Indigenous People, the Convention on the Elimination of Discrimination against Women and the Yogyakarta Principles all identify quite clearly for us the relationship between non- discrimination and liberty, the non negotiability of both, and the indispensability of the exercise of due diligence by state actors to prevent derogations entrenched in discriminatory social contexts. General Recommendation 19 of CEDAW on violence against women for instance states: "The definition of discrimination includes gender based violence, that is violence that is directed against a woman because she is a woman or that affects women disproportionately. It includes acts that inflict physical, mental or sexual harm or suffering, threats of such acts, coercion and other deprivations of liberty."[8]

Legislations and case law have recognized the centrality of international conventions notably the Persons with Disabilities Act, 1995, the Protection of Women from Domestic Violence Act, 2005, the Vishakha decision[9], the Naz Foundation[10] decision, to name a few. New social movements focusing on disability rights, dalit rights, minority rights, adivasi rights, women's rights and the rights of LGBT communities have used these conventions to combat public morality in governance and civil society.

The idea of non-discrimination, I argue is distinct from the idea of equality, and cannot be reduced to an expression of or a sub-set of the equality principle. In suggesting this, I draw from the decision of the minority in Kharak Singh,[11] which was later affirmed in a series of judgments including Maneka Gandhi, that Article 19 and Article 21 are independent fundamental rights, which overlap and are not mutually exclusive. It is important to develop this view further to say that each fundamental right in the constitution is independent and interdependent that no fundamental right can be seen as being carved out of another, or as being a sub-set of another.

Although "[t]he attempt of the Court should be to expand the reach and ambit of the fundamental rights rather than attenuate their meaning and content by a process of judicial construction," scholarship and jurisprudence on non-discrimination has tended to be restricted and reductionist, viewing the important right to non-discrimination as a mere facet of equality (See Seervai 435-692). To take one thread of equality jurisprudence in India, if arbitrariness is antithetical to equality and therefore a violation of Article 14, it takes the opposite route in the case of non-discrimination where the derogation of the right is accomplished not through arbitrariness in state action but through a systematic, planned and systemic deployment of power in an organized fashion horizontally (between classes inter se) and vertically (by the state) to.divest communities/ classes of the right to liberty. Discrimination is not contained by the "arbitrariness" principle (delineated at length in Maneka Gandhi) in interpretation and therefore cannot be seen as a subset of equality alone.

On the other hand, "arbitrariness" acquires an amplified meaning if understood from the standpoint of non-discrimination. Any reading of any part of the constitutional guarantee of non-discrimination that truncates its meaning may be said to be arbitrary because it interprets the right against itself and thereby negates it. The "basic structure" doctrine safeguards the constitution from any abridgement through legislative amendment. This safeguard would render any jurisprudential/interpretive abridgement impermissible. I have attempted to demonstrate through a close reading of case law the specific ways in which the doctrine of permissible classification often foregrounds discriminatory practices even while it guides equality jurisprudence. Would it then be apt to turn the formulation of the relationship between Article 14 and Article 15 around to say that it is the principle of non discrimination that comes into play where it concerns group indices like sex, race, caste, place of birth and religion, rather than the principle of equality? Article 15 recognises in substantive terms that groups are unequally placed and that this has physical and material consequences on the groups located at the bottom of the social order. It also recognises that there are several simultaneous channels of deployment of discrimination.

A layered application of the principle of non-discrimination, which progresses from the simple enunciation of equality (Article 14), through significant elements of difference and plurality (Article 15), to the deployment of coercion and force (Articles 17, 21 and 23) roughens up the smooth and flat terrain of equality, and enables a more comprehensive appreciation of the principle of non discrimination.

> These fundamental rights represent the basic values cherished by the people of this country…It is apparent from the enunciation of these rights that the respect for the individual and his capacity for individual volition which finds expression there is not a self- fulfilling prophecy. Its purpose is to help the individual to find his own liability, to give expression to his creativity and to prevent governmental and other forces from 'alienating' the individual from his creative impulses.

Initially this project began as an attempt to map the "distinct" fields of discrimination set out in Article 15 and explore the relation of each field to the question of liberty as set out in Article 21 of the Constitution of India. The primary distinction was between "common" fields (like gender and disability) and "discrete" ones (religion, tribe, caste).

As each field began to open out, however, this neat classification was immediately thrown into crisis because (a) within the common fields there are glaring invisibilisations ("denotified tribes", women with intellectual disabilities, transgender persons, for instance) that remained separate, isolated and excluded within larger political and juridical/legal articulations; (b) the categories that were presumed to be discrete showed up connections not only with the common categories of gender and disability (which are anticipated in the formulation) but between so-called discrete categories that no longer remained separate and distinct.

The intersection of caste with religion; tribe with caste; tribe with religion; religion with caste; religion with tribe; the intersection of class with each of the categories and combinations of categories, produced a mosaic of plurality saturated with power that the guarantees of non discrimination and liberty needed to reach out to. This in a situation where governmentality and juridicalisation have historically tended to impose homogeneity, a construct that served the ideological function of defining normativity outside of the lived experience.

Extending Maneka Gandhi, I would argue that any attempt to examine the different sites of non-discrimination and liberty must be guided by the view that "the tests of reason and justice cannot be abstract. [They] have to be pragmatic" and must evolve new interpretive protocols and strategies to grasp the complexity of the problem at hand. These involve, importantly the amplification of interpretive tools that have been devised in or in relation to courts, but have been confined to a specific application.

Moving away from a disaggregated approach to understanding non- discrimination and liberty adopting instead a holistic, cross sectoral, intersectional approach that looks at connections and possibilities that might enrich the scope of non-discrimination – involves a shift that forces a re-examination of a range of materials hitherto inadequately explored in constitutional jurisprudence and legal research on non- discrimination.

This shift draws on the delineation of the "basic structure of the constitution" set out in Kesavananda Bharathi :

> "The basic structure may be said to consist of the following features :
>
> (1) Supremacy of the Constitution;
> (2) Republican and Democratic form of Government
> (3) Secular character of the Constitution;
> (4) Separation of powers between the Legislature, the executive and the judiciary;
> (5) Federal character of the Constitution.
>
> The above structure is built on the basic foundation, i.e., the dignity and freedom of the individual. This is of supreme importance. This cannot by any form of amendment be destroyed.

> The above foundation and the above basic features are easily discernible not only from the preamble but the whole scheme of the Constitution."

The standard interpretation of Article 15 (1) has given undue weight to the word "only" while not considering the jurisprudential implications of the concluding phrase "or any of them" which might open out radical possibilities for the interpretation of non discrimination. Proceeding on the assumption that the constitution can contain no surplusage, and that all words and phrases are intended to convey meaning, a re-examination of Article 15 leads us to conclude that the concluding phrase of the first clause, "or any of them" enables a consideration of intersectionality in non discrimination jurisprudence, that need not any more be limited to one of the stated indices alone.

While in legal usage the word "only" in this context denotes "solely" (Garner 1987, 390) and this is the way it has been interpreted by courts in India, there is no discussion either in the Constituent Assembly or in case law on the concluding phrase of this clause "or any of them" (Rao 1968, 182-192). The word "or" in legal usage means both "and" and "or" (Garner 1987, 394). Opening this clause out and re-examining its import, points us in a different direction: namely, the state shall not discriminate solely on the listed grounds, and on any of the listed grounds in the singular or the plural, and on grounds of any of the listed indices with factors that do not figure in this list factors that allude to the larger context. The word "only" by this token need not drive a wedge between biological sex and socially constructed gender for instance as Martha Nussbaum argues.

The idea of hostile environments is critical to an understanding of the interlocking of discrimination and curtailment of liberty. From relatively 'benign' forms of harassment and hate speech against dalits, adivasis, muslims, women, sexual minorities and the differently abled to incarceration, assault and atrocity, and further to the dis-abling of legal redress and remedy, hostile environments are entrenched in contexts of discrimination and have an immediate negative effect on the exercise of the right to liberty by communities/ classes that are targets of discrimination. Looking at liberty in relation to hostile environments also revalorizes liberty itself beyond the limiting scope of individual liberty, which is always theoretically available in our society, but practically far out of reach.

Eliminating hostile environments and setting the standards of non-discrimination, is possible through the exercise of due diligence by the state. Although the principle of Due Diligence is set out in international conventions like the CEDAW as indispensable to the realization of non-discrimination, the SR Sankaran Government Orders on untouchability demonstrate ways in which this principle might be operationalised and accomplished. These GOs also anticipate the enunciation of this principle in international law, and point to the possibility that international human rights law draws on strategies developed through the diligent local application of constitutional morality, just as it does on philosophies of justice that are rooted in the local.

Finally, the problem of violence. The interlocking of discrimination with the loss of liberty is fundamentally violent in context and process. In looking at both violence and the operation of the law, what is striking is the ways in which struggles for human rights and civil liberties especially have taught us to use institutions of justice, the courts especially, creatively, to wrest political rights in a democracy. The influence of these struggles is immediately apparent in jurisprudence as well, with courts having to reckon with subaltern constitutionalism, which "crystallizes [a multitudinous register of diverse] citizen practices of reimaging democracy, politics, and the fullness of democratic citizenship."

The tools for subaltern constitutionalism have been crafted in courts, by the bureaucracy and by legislatures in response to subaltern resistance. It would not therefore be accurate to posit this idea in opposition to spaces that are vested with the authority to set out or interpret the law within the framework of the constitution. Nevertheless, it is also true that on a balance, the legislature, executive and judiciary are too often weighed against marginalized communities and subaltern politics. What this project attempts to map therefore is constitutional law's Other subaltern constitutionalism. This Other is located sometimes within the fields of constitutional law judicial and administrative, sometimes within trial courts which ironically maintain a hierarchical distance from constitutional courts, and sometimes in the heart of popular struggles.

Any project that attempts to grapple with the idea of a transformative constitutionalism must by definition spill over boundaries. However, most often, research and writing on discrimination has focused on a single aspect. This is especially true of legal scholarship (See Crenshaw 1989). Notwithstanding significant shifts, the problem of discrimination is rendered more complex by the fact that institutional apparatuses – panchayats, policing, courts, prison administration and forensic science in India exclude marginal communities/classes quite literally. The discursive formations that emerge from this structure, not unexpectedly, tend to be exclusionary.

Sociological scholarship is yet to address itself to the problem of discrimination in all its complexity. Again, it has tended to focus narrowly on a specific aspect, and has not begun to engage with the constitution or the law in the analysis of discrimination. Further, the corpus of sociology and social anthropology that focuses on aspects of discrimination is constructed in deeply problematic ways that infiltrate the jurisprudence on non-discrimination that draws on this corpus.

An important part of this work has been to demonstrate the possibility of reconstructing the corpus of materials legal and sociological – on non-discrimination. While acknowledging the pitfalls of grand theory (Mills 1959) and grand narratives (Douzinas et. al. 1991), understanding the scope of constitutionalism in contemporary Indian society requires the crafting of analytical tools and methods that enable an understanding of issues within a large canvas. Further, while specialisations certainly facilitate a richer critical engagement with problems of marginality and exclusion, as also diversity, a specific, single focus approach to the study of non-discrimination results in problems that are both theoretical and practical it is in looking at the problems of disability, caste, tribe, religion and gender and the diversities within each that we get a clearer view of the constitutional project of non-discrimination in its entirety. This also, at the level of practical engagement, facilitates the conceptualization of alliances between anti-discrimination struggles.

This methodological and pedagogical shift merits some elaboration. In making meaning of diverse sources, each with its own established interpretive protocols, it is important to move away from the "doctrinal," "precedent" driven approaches that are common to both sociology and constitutional interpretation, because these established modes of reading texts prescribe strict limits to the act of reading and the possibilities for interpretation that such reading will yield. Instead, crossing genres and tracing the haziness of boundaries, reading against the grain and mapping the fault lines in the way justice figures in the dominant imaginary as well as in institutions entrusted with the "delivery of justice," enables a different construction of the legal and sociological corpus.

The difficulty however, is in the fact that both the legal and sociological materials are uneven across these categories. While for instance, the historical materials on gender and caste is rich and varied, the search for different materials on tribes yields uneven results with a concentration on the colonial period, historiographies of disability remain to be written, while the sociology of disability in India is only now beginning to draw the attention of scholars. This unevenness is reflected in the attempt to piece together an intellectual history of non-discrimination. An intersectional approach across different indices of discrimination enables an understanding of one in relation to another, synchronizing the intersectional interpretive method suggested in the reading of Article 15(1) with an interweaving of intellectual histories in understanding patterns of discrimination. This also has the potential of enriching our understanding of the scope of analogous grounds of discrimination, which involves the application in jurisprudence of precisely this method of reading texts. On a more general level, this method identifies quite easily for us the gaps in materials pointing to possibilities of future research.

The worrying easy recourse to public morality, jurisprudential dissociation and the truncated, disaggregated reading of the constitution by constitutional courts, in this context, needs to be ceaselessly resisted by its Other, within and outside courts so that "a social and economic revolution can gradually take place while preserving the freedom and dignity of every citizen." Transformative constitutionalism that is based on the subaltern experience is necessary in order for non-discrimination and liberty to blossom as incontrovertible constitutional guarantees and in order for constitutional morality to actually pave the way for "notional change" and social transformation.

References

1. Ambedkar, B.R. [1948] 2002. Basic features of the Indian constitution. In *The Essential Writings of B.R. Ambedkar.* Ed Rodrigues, Valerian. Delhi, Oxford University Press, 2002, 473-494.
2. Bauman, Zygmunt [1988] 1997. *Freedom.* Delhi, World View.
3. Brinda Bose and Subhabrata Bhattacharyya, eds. *The phobic and the erotic : The politics of sexualities in contemporary India,* Seagull Books (London, New York, Calcutta).
4. Brown, Wendy 2001. *Politics out of history.* Princeton and Oxford, Princeton University Press.
5. Brown, Wendy 2006. *Regulating aversion: Tolerance in the age of identity and empire.* Princeton and Oxford, Princeton University Press.
6. Butler, Judith, Spivak, Gayatri Chakravorty 2007. *Who sings the nation state? Language, politics, belonging.* Calcutta, Seagull Books.
7. Guha, Ranajit 1983. *Elementary aspects of peasant insurgency in colonial India.* Delhi : Oxford University Press.
8. Rawls, John [1971] 1999. *A Theory of Justice.* Oxford : Oxford University Press. Sen, Amartya 2009. The Idea of Justice. London:Allen Lane.
9. Skinner, Quentin, 1998. *Liberty before liberalism.* Cambridge, Cambridge University Press.
10. Supiot, Alain 2007. *Homo juridicus : On the anthropological function of the law.* Trans. Saskia Brown. Verso : London.
11. Zwilling, Leonard, and Sweet, Michael J. 2000. *The evolution of third-sex constructs in ancient India : A study in ambiguity. In Invented identities : The interplay of gender, religion and politics in India.* Eds. Leslie, Julia and McGee, Mary. New Delhi, Oxford University Press, 99-132.

Idea of The Hindi Heartland

Shaibal Gupta

Ideating the Lecture

One sultry afternoon in Patna, couple of weeks back, when Professor Pradeep Bhargava, Director of the G.B. Pant Social Science Institute, rang me inviting me to deliver this year's G.B. Pant Memorial Lecture, I thought he must have dialed a wrong number. With trepidations, I had to dial a common friend who had introduced me to Professor Bhargava, to confirm the authenticity of the invitation. It is indeed an immense honour for me to have been given the opportunity to deliver a lecture in memory of one of the foremost freedom fighters and the builder of modern India, Pandit Govind Ballabh Pant. Pandit Pant, besides being a freedom fighter, had also choreographed the development of the post- independent India, first as the Chief Minister of Uttar Pradesh and later as a Union Home Minister. Apart from the honour of delivering the memorial lecture in the name of an outstanding Indian icon, a visit to the G.B. Pant Social Science Institute is a must academic pilgrimage to the historic city of Allahabad. Allahabad is situated at the confluence of three rivers Ganga, Yamuna and Saraswati, two real and one possibly mythical; in contrast, the G.B. Pant Social Science Institute has been the convergence point of ideas, idealism and ideals, all of them real, representing the best of traditions of human civilization. This could be possible because the Institute is nestled in a city which was the epicenter of the cosmopolitan culture of India and home of Pandit Jawaharlal Nehru.

Idea of The Hindi Heartland, 10th September, 2014, G.B. Pant Social Science Institute

Not being a professional teacher, deciding on the topic of a lecture in memory of a formidable historical personality, was a challenging experience for me. It was further exuberated by Professor Bhargava, who gave me a freehand on the choice of topic. He was also generous enough to suggest that I could limit my delivery to Bihar or any topic of my choice. The first option would entail that I would not venture into an unknown territory. On the other hand, his munificence in allowing me an unfettered option gave me an opportunity to transcend beyond my benighted province and my immediate cognitive world. But while transcending beyond the immediate cognitive world, one is often conditioned by some cataclysmic factors that decisively invade your cognitive world. One such cataclysm was an innocuous report in the Patna edition of the Times of India of August 10, 2014 that the Government of India has ordered "5 Bharat Ratna medallions from the RBI mint."[1]

This has fuelled "speculation in political circles that Bharat Ratna beneficiaries this year will be more than one."[2] Apart from two highly expected recipients, Atal Bihari Vajpayee and Netaji Subhas Chandra Bose, the report further indicates that "the feeling in the Sangh Parivar is that the charismatic nationalist never got his due, with successive governments keen to ensure that the spotlight remained on the Nehru-Gandhi family. Many in Sangh Parivar also feel that it was high time that Madan Mohan Malviya, founder of the Benaras Hindu University (BHU), got it. Their list of suggested beneficiaries also include Hanuman Prasad Poddar, founder of the Gita Press, who popularized Hindu epics, along with the legendary painter Raja Ravi Varma, considered to have done for Hinduism what Gutenberg Press did for Bible."[3] Another news report of the Patna edition of Times of India of August 28 was a reassuring one, which reported that "President Pranab Mukherjee on Wednesday gave awards to 28 persons, including three journalists and an ISRO scientist, for their outstanding contribution towards development and spread of Hindi".[4] The most redeeming feature of the ceremony was that the first award was distributed in the name of Dr. George Grierson for spread of Hindi in foreign lands; the second Atmaram Award for writings in Hindi on scientific and technical subjects; the third Rahul Sankrityayan Award for research in Hindi and travelogues;

and the fourth Ganesh Shanker Vidyarthi Award for contribution to Hindi journalism. Incidentally, these awards were constituted several decades ago by the then Government of India. While the speculations on the possible Bharat Ratna recipient were furiously debated in the electronic and print media, Union Government conceded that the minimum requirement of English proficiency is no longer required for prelims of CSAT examination. This was another cataclysm for me. This was in response to the prolonged agitation by Hindi-speaking students of the country, against the norm of the UPSC for the civil services examination. This decision of the present Union Government was not liked by the intelligentsia in South India. In a signed article, S.L. Rao a pro-market columnist and fairly well disposed towards the possible demise of the Congress party in the 2014 parliamentary election, wrote in The Telegraph that "this government's Hindi-centric attitudes led to a bad compromise with agitating 'students' against the UPSC examination system. It devalues the test for admission to India's 'steel frame'. The agitation really targets the tests in English and basic analytical skills. It opens the door to a revival of the anti-Hindi agitation that almost tore the country apart a few decades ago. This government is overwhelmingly Hindi-speaking. It strikes no chords, specially in South India."[5] He went on to add that "with the Hindi dominance, we can expect agitations to increase in the pro-Hindi states. Reactions will follow in non-Hindi states. Three months of the Modi government signals capture by the RSS, bureaucracy and the Hindi Heartland".[6]

This decision of the Union Government was also not liked by Professor Alok Rai, the grandson of Munshi Prem Chand, an eminent littérateur himself, who always wanted value addition in the language endowment. Rai regretted that "predictably, politicians have won".[7]

He opined that "educationally the most appropriate response … would be not to lower the bar but to raise it higher … by adding another compulsory 'vernacular' language component to the CSAT. The urban Anglophone would be required to demonstrate competence in any one Indian language of her choice, other than English. This would, at one stroke, eliminate the advantage of the urban English-monolingual. Indeed, the vernacular component — Hindi or Bengali or Tamil—can also be so devised as to eliminate those whose vernacular competence goes little beyond ordering their servants."[8] After capturing the Hindi Heartland, there is a concerted strategy to "expand its footprint in the rest of the country",[9] opined Kalyani Shanker, an avidly pro-Congress columnist. The concern about the domination of Hindi and its capacity to forestall the growth of other languages are not of recent origin. Paul Brass, who followed Hindi Heartland very closely, wrote several decades ago that the "wolf of Hindi" has not been entirely unsuccessful in north Bihar".[10] The majority of the people living there are not aware that Maithili is their mother tongue, even though it independently had vibrant cultural, geographical, ethnic and language construct. Incidentally, contempt for thc 'vernacular language', on the other hand, has got internalized in the psyche of the Indian elite. Otherwise, a senior academic would not have confided to Professor Yogendra Yadav, ideologue of the youngest political party of India, that "languages like Hindi and Tamil are good for street conversation. But surely you cannot do conceptual thinking in these languages the way you can in English and French".[11]

The import of both the cataclysms has unsettled me from the narrow confines of my cognitive world and led me to my "tryst" with the wider "Idea of the Hindi Heartland". Had Pandit Govind Ballabh Pant been alive, I wonder how he would have grappled with the current agenda, as Hindi was not only an integral part of his cognitive world, he had indeed established its authority in the country. Not only he gave shape to the movement for Hindi as a Union Home Minister, he also promoted its increased use as the official language. It is he who ensured that the merit list of the candidates in UPSC examination will be prepared on the basis of the marks obtained jointly in the written examination and the interview. Earlier, one had to compete separately. This decision of the Union Home Ministry ensured that a large number of candidates with "vernacular" proficiency could succeed in the UPSC examination. They were generally disadvantaged earlier in the interview, in the absence of their proficiency in English.

Making of Hindi Heartland's Society

In this backdrop, I want to calibrate on the "Idea of the Hindi Heartland". Is it a tangible concept or is it in the realm of speculation only? Is it a geographical expression alone or also a coherent cultural construct? In either case, is it a "contemptuous" specification or otherwise? Why the tectonic shift in the national ruling political configuration is being considered as a capture by the Hindi Heartland? Why Hindi Heartland has suddenly come to the centre stage?

To answer all these questions, one may first note that since the independence, the contour and complexion of the Union Government has generally been decided in the electoral field of the Hindi Heartland. Independence movement against the colonial rule was also won in the "playing fields" of the Hindi Heartland. Even the diabolic roots of the vivisection of the country in 1947 were worked out in this region. Most of the Prime Ministers of India, after independence, were from the Hindi Heartland. Amplification of the Hindi Heartland is so preponderant that even the leaders from the region with limited electoral capital are often considered to be the shadow Prime Ministers. In this backdrop, one wonders why Hindi Heartland is being suddenly singled out as a distinctive, geographical, cultural and ideological construct. The idea of Southern states indicates certain brand. Bengal was once considered to be the ultimate brand. Remember Gopal Krishna Gokhle who had once said "What Bengal thinks today, India thinks tomorrow and rest of the world day after"[12]; but Gokhle will be turning in his grave now in the backdrop of the present pathetic condition of the state. Ironically, at present, neither the Prime Minister nor the President of the national ruling party is from the Hindi Heartland; both were born after independence and thus do not carry the institutional memory of the freedom movement. Yet there is a larger-than-life hegemony being established about the Hindi Heartland.

The Idea of Hindi Heartland is wider now than its geographical expanse. Earlier, the idea was ephemeral and its geography was uncharted in India. Unlike most of the countries in Europe, India is too large a country to be a homogeneous one with respect to either physical or economic or social characteristics. That the country is still a single political unit is indeed creditworthy; but this also sometimes misleads people to be oblivious of the wide social divergences within the country. Bihar, Madhya Pradesh, Rajasthan, Uttar Pradesh, Jharkhand, Chhattisgarh and Uttarakhand these seven states form one region where both social and economic progress have been the least. Surprisingly, the linguistic base of all these seven states is Hindi, which is the official language of the country. With the adoption of the Indian Constitution in 1950, Hindi (in Devnagri script) was accepted as the official language of the country. Contrary to the general misconception, Hindi is not the national language of the country.[13] As per the Census data, Hindi is the mother tongue of 22 percent of the population of the country, but spoken as a language by 42 percent of its population. Once the Constitution of India came into force on January 26, 1950, the "status of Hindi was greatly enhanced".[14]

The documentation of Linguistic Survey of India by George Abraham Grierson "played very important role in the life of Hindi and in the life of India".[15] Grierson opined that Hindi "popularly applied to all the various Aryan languages spoken between the Punjab on the west and the river Mahananda on the east; and between the Himalayas on the north and the river Narmada on the south".[16] The Hindi language includes 49 mother tongues, "creating a statistical majority. If this kind of clustering is not done, the linguistic demography of Hindi will be different".[17]

The 1911 Census of India considers Hindi as a "comprehensive word which includes at least three distinct languages, Western Hindi, Eastern Hindi and Bihari".[18] 'Hindustani' was major component of Hindi, popularly known as "Bazaar Hindi", "more akin to Mahatma Gandhi's notion".[19] When Hindi was deconstructed, Eastern Hindi consisted of Awadhi, Maithili, Magahi and Bhojpuri; Western Hindi consisted of Urdu, Braj Bhasa; and Bihari and Rajasthani were stand alone languages. Incidentally, Uttar Pradesh declared Hindi in Devanagari script as its official language on October 8, 1947 and, in the same month, notified that Hindi be used in the civil and criminal courts. Similarly, Bihar adopted Hindi as the official language on June 4, 1948 and on June 26, declared it as the language of the court.[20] In Uttar

Pradesh and Bihar, Hindi had to compete with the "justified" claims of Awadhi, Braj Bhasa, Urdu, Bhojpuri, Magahi and Maithili to occupy the linguistic space of the state. My "Idea" of the Hindi Heartland will be mainly around Bihar, Uttar Pradesh, Rajasthan and Madhya Pradesh.

The essential brand or idea about the Hindi Heartland has generally been considered as conservative in India, although it has been the home of some of the foremost progressive litterateurs and journalists like Premchand[21], Phanishwar Nath Renu[22], Surya Kant Tripathi 'Nirala'[23], Firaq Gorakhpuri[24], Baba Nagarjun[25], Mahadevi Verma[26], Hazari Prasad Diwedi[27], Ramvriksha Benipuri[28], Ramvilas Sharma[29], Harishankar Parsai[30], Sharad Joshi[31], Krishna Chander[32], Yashpal[33], Rahul Sankrityayan[34], Ganesh Shanker Vidyarthi[35] and others. Simultaneously, Bihar and Uttar Pradesh were also the bastion of powerful socialist, communist and radical movements. Even Madhya Pradesh and Rajasthan had pockets of socialist and communist influence. The peasant movement in Bihar and Eastern Uttar Pradesh was the response to the "Permanent Settlement" that was introduced by Lord Cornwallis way back in 1793 in these areas. Swami Sahajanand Saraswati's concern, initially for the Bhumihar tenant in Bihar led to the concern for the general tenant later, which contributed to the scripting of the socialist and communist formations. He was also a fierce critique of the ante-diluvian Brahminical social order, and prepared a foundation for several progressive leaders of the Hindi Heartland. He had also substantial influence in Uttar Pradesh, specially in its eastern part. Apart from the contribution of the libertarian littérateur and radical movement, Jawarharlal Nehru from the mainstream politics and P.C. Joshi from the communist movement tried to construct the "identity" and the "idea" of the Hindi Heartland, breaking its traditional conservative image. Over and above, the powerful foundation of the dedicated socialist movement were laid in the Hindi Heartland by Acharya Narendra Dev, Ram Manohar Lohia, Jay Prakash Narayan, Karpoori Thakur and others. They had also contributed to the brand building of the Hindi Heartland. In spite of such a powerful cosmopolitan and left tradition, the baggage of history has been a serious impediment towards a democratic construct of the region. This was partly because the first major resistance to the colonial rule was made in this region (during the First War of Independence in 1857) and, ever since then, the British exploitation has been the most severe here. As a result, while regions like Bengal and Maharashtra had taken to English-education and certain social reforms much earlier, people in Hindi Heartland have persistently resisted such attempts, viewing them as colonial strategies to destroy their own culture and tradition.

The pre-mutiny liberalism had given way to a paternalism which had little use for either the conservative romantic attachment to the peasantry, or the liberal desire to educate the middle class, with which it had formerly been prepared to share power to some extent".[36]

This has led to the "reformist spirit of the thirties that had acquired a strong and undisguisedly racist tone after 1857".[37]

The Arya Samaj also played an important role against English education. Its founder Dayanand Saravati felt, that "English education is vehicle for conversion to Christanity".[38] He has been "sensitive to the use and potential as a community language of Hindi, which he called the aryabhasa, the language of the Aryans".[39]

In the absence of the liberal space, a reverse ideological anchor was weaved around "Hindu, Hindi, Hindustan". This slogan first appeared in the journal 'Brahman', edited by Pratapnarayan Mishra, in the later part of the nineteenth century, after the First War of Independence in 1857. In the closing issue of the Journal, in the absence of resources to continue its printing, he wrote : "If you truly desire your own welfare, then keep chanting the mantra with one tongue **Hindu, Hindi, Hindustan**, whether it attracts or repels the world, brings respect or affront, don't leave of chanting with one voice **Hindu, Hindi, Hindustan**; those who don't know their own identity are like the living dead, so sing loud this mantra **Hindi, Hindu, Hindustan**; wise are those who don't discard their own language, food and clothing in all its proof of good fortune - **Hindi, Hindu, Hindustan**".[40]

Bharatendu Harischandra, the father of modern Hindi literature, essentially coopted the ideological construct of his contemporary and friend Pratapnarayan Mishra and created an "informed public opinion and the constituents of Hindu/Indian national identity. Language, literature, religion, territorial allegiance were all aspects of being Hindu".[41]

Mystique Triad of Brahmins, Benaras and Banias

Just as the ideological epicenter of the 'Young Bengal' movement was 'Calcutta', 'Banaras' emerged as the academic and ideological, alternative centre of gravity of the Hindi Heartland. In addition to the effect of the British Raj, the Arya Samaj Movement too reinforced the "varna" system. Subsequently, Bharatendu Harishchandra added to the appeal and credibility of caste orthodoxy. He was backed by the authority of the holy city of Benaras, the citadel of a new merchant aristocracy led by the Maharaja of Banaras, the traditional base of Sanskrit learning and Brahmin "punditry". Bharatendu coined an apparently paradoxical "new traditionalist idiom" and effectively heralded the use of modern print media to initiate and direct change. The intellectual catchment area of the Hindu orthodoxy of Benaras was the entire Hindi Heartland.[42]

The triad of Brahmin Pandits, merchants of Benaras and the King of Benaras created the ideological foundation of the Hindi Heartland. Benaras was self-consciously Hindu city; it had a Hindu Maharaja, a Hindu merchant class, and a Hindu priestly order, although it was administered by the British. Consequently, the region had failed to give rise to an enlightened middle class, who in most other parts of the country had spearheaded the social reforms and the incentive consciousness for production and productivity.

The citadel of Benaras, main trigger of ideological conservatism, was considered to be the foremost seat of ritualistic and traditional learning. This was in itself a part of the Puranic tradition coined by the Brahmans who, in turn, coined their own self perception. "In spite of the repeated destruction of the major temples, Kashi remained a vital religious meeting point under the Delhi sultans and the Mughal emperors. The Brahmans and their institutions had enjoyed the patronage of the Rajputs and merchants throughout the period of the Delhi sultanate and the Mughals. In the late Mughal period, the Marathas had practically replaced the patronage by the Rajputs".[43] During the British period, colonial administration in the process of patronage "wanted in turn to profit from the Brahmin authority".[44] Way back in 1791, Benaras Sanskrit college was founded by them for "endearing to ...the native Hindoos".[45] Thus, the cognitive world of the Brahmin was not only the Hindi Heartland but the entire constituency of Hindustan. This could become possible because of the varying constituency of Brahmins from the different states and, in the process, the authority of the pan- Indian Hindu ritualistic constituency could be established. According to Asiatic Researches in 1832, Brahmans constituted 12 percent of the city's population, with Maharastrian Brahmans outnumbering the rest; the latter constituted 30 per cent of the total Brahman population. Earlier, with the fall of the Vijayanagar in the sixteenth century, "Brahmans from the south began to pour into the city".[46]

Next to the Brahmins, the second most important constituent of the triad was the King of Benaras. Even though he was the titular head of the holy city, he came to hold great symbolic power. With the ascendance of the British over the years, "the political control of the region was soon to pass from their hands".[47] Once they were marginalized politically and administratively, they actively intervened in the religious affairs. In the process, they ensured "immense public presence, and it was their religious and cultural authority that created the representational public arena in festivities such as the river festival of Burhva Mangal and the month-long Ramlila.[48] In the framework provided by these public occasions that they most effectively registered their kingly presence. In the Ramlila, they presented "themselves as representative of this deity, thus deliberately setting forth the Puranic tradition of the city".[49] The patronage of the kings, "reinforced by merchant money, of Sanskrit learning, bhasa poetry and music, which made for the specifically Hindu culture of Benaras as it evolved in the nineteenth century".[50]

The third element in the triad the merchants of Benaras also played a decisive role in the super structural construction of the Hindi Heartland. Unlike in other parts of the Hindi Heartland, the Banias, the main social base of the merchants of Benaras, were almost at par with the "Pandits" or "Kings" in terms of authority and social status. This could become possible because "Benaras itself became one of the fastest growing cities in the years during 1750-90, the virtual inland commercial capital of the subcontinent after the decline of Murshidabad and the collapse of the Jagat Seths in Bengal in 1734".[51]

The creation of the Mint in 1734, relatively stable agriculture around the city, and the presence of large sums of bullion or credit in the city, made it attractive for the East India Company to make full use of its commercial facilities. By the 1780s, the Benaras region had become the commercial and financial cross-roads for the whole of the subcontinent. "There were strong links and continuities between the pre-colonial formation of business communities and the communities that exercised financial control through the earlier colonial period. As far as the pattern of merchant intervention and mediation was concerned... most of them Hindu, occupied the vital intermediary position as financial and diplomatic guarantees to the various local chiefs and zamindars".[52] Like Brahmans, the professional merchants in Benaras were also not a homogeneous community. They were from all over the country, including some from Gujarat. The heterogeneous group of local traders, dominated by the vaishyas, also consisted of the rising families of lower castes such as telis (oil pressers) or kalvar (liquor distillers). The category of merchant might have accounted for about 20 per cent of the population of the city, if small-time traders were also included. It was largely from the ranks of the merchants then that the agitation for the recognition of Hindi as the language of the courts was carried out, making Allahabad and Benaras the joint centres of the Hindi movement. "The most prominent merchants participated actively in the Maharaja's Dharma Sabha, the activities of which were recorded from the late sixties of the nineteenth century, and it was the Vaishnava sampradayas of the merchants, foremost the Vallabha sampradaya, which formed the core of the traditionalist rearticulation of Hinduism".[53] Contrary to the general character of the social movement in south and western India and Bengal proper, which normally emerged as a critique of the Brahminical system, Banaras experienced a different social dynamics. The Brahmin hegemony "strongly dominated the cultural scene in Benaras in the early nineteenth century, being generously supported both by the raja and the merchants. It was indeed established in the late Mughal period by the rapidly expanding Marathas. The catchment area of the Hindu orthodoxy was not limited to the Hindi Heartland, but had extended to southern and western India as well. Infact, Benaras was the "celestial home" of the orthodox Brahmins from south and western India as well. It was, therefore, not a political accident that Narendra Modi decided to contest from Benaras; he was trying to send a religious message across the Hindu constituency of India in general and the Hindi Heartland in particular. The agenda of Narendra Modi did not end with getting elected from the city; he is now in the process of building an enviable brand of "Benaras" globally, which will cater to the Hindu diaspora, as well. Thus one of the key elements of the recent visit of Prime Minister to Japan is to forge a "partner city affiliation between Kyoto and Varanasi".[54] Kyoto was not only imperial capital of Japan and home to Buddhist shrines, but the best example of heritage conservation and city modernization, cooperating on culture, art and academics. Narendra Modi wants to make Benaras the "spiritual capital of India".[55] The city, known for its temple, colourful river aartis and cremation ghats, is in crying need of modernization, but without losing any of its character.

While they have convincingly co-opted the upper and lower backwards in the Hindi Heartland, The Telegraph of September 7, 2014 reports that there is now an "RSS bid to woo Dalits"[56]. The Telegraph further report, that "RSS chief Mohanrao Bhagwat will... launch a three volume work in Hindi on the 'Hindu' identity of India's Dalits...Union Minister Smriti Irani and Prakash Javadkar will be special guests, signifying the Sangh parivar's agenda to 'reclaim' the 'Hindu roots' of Schedule castes"[57]. The works, authored by Bizay Sonkar Shastri are about three major Dalit castes Jatavs, Valmikis and Khatiks. Interestingly, the titles of the sub-castes has been pre-fixed with the word 'Hindu'. For example, Jatavs are referred in the book as 'Hindu Charmakar Jati'. Along with high valued pre-fixing, their past is also being reinvented. In the book on the Valmikis, Shastri writes that "they were born as ...Brahmins and Kshatriyas who were turned into scavengers when outsiders invaded India. The infidels saw...(them) as their main threats"[58]. In some sense, therefore, the RSS has possibly a better sense of history and would not like the replication of mistake of Joginder Nath Mandal, the first Chairman of Constituent Assembly of Pakistan and also its first Law Minister. He was the leader of the Dalit of Bengal and the social trauma that Dalits had to face in Bengal had led him to opt for Pakistan.

Incidentally, he vacated his seat for the Constituent Assembly for Dr. B.R. Ambedkar, who later became its Chairman and drafted the Indian Constitution. Inspite of the so called 'renaissance' in Bengal prior to independence, the cooption of the Dalits by the 'Bhadrolok' was far from a reality there. The tyranny has been so preponderant that the Dalit leader even with deep roots opted for Pakistan. In the post-independence India again, the 'public policy' on mainstreaming Dalits has not been very successful. Karl Marx had rightly said that "History repeats itself, first as tragedy, second as farce".

Identity Issue in Hindi Heartland

In the backdrop of Brahmin-centric religious and social construction, the process of multi-caste social movement could not usher in this part of the country. In those parts of the country which experienced any social reform, it was either the caste or the national identity that acted as the immediate impetus for "self identity". Thanks to the enormous socio-cultural divergence across the country, each state in India has multiple identities. Language is probably the most dominant or visible dimension of that identity and literacy plays a major role in promoting a language-based identity. But unlike in Bengal proper and many other states of the Indian Union, even the radical and progressive intelligentsia of the Hindi Heartland was not generally associated with the literacy movement. In Bengal proper, it was personalities like Ishwar Chandra Vidyasagar or Rabindra Nath Tagore who were pioneers in promoting Bengali language and thereby strengthening Bengali identity. Both scripted primers for the Bengali language.

The concept of a social region rests not only on certain common social practices that its inhabitants may share, but on the acquisition of a regional identity as well. Since India is too large a country, inhabited by people of various religions and languages in diverse geographical areas, the emergence of a national identity here has often been accompanied by a simultaneous emergence of regional identity. The process of the emergence of nationalism in India had started during the British period, basically as a reaction to the colonial presence. But, because of the socio-cultural diversity of its people, nationalism has been developing here at two levels one at all-India on the basis of pan- Indian cultural homogeneity and anti-imperialism and another at regional level, generally around a linguistic identity. One could afford to be a Tamil, Marathi, Gujrati or Bengali, as well as a very nationalist Indian. It is no accident that the two songs of Rabindra Nath Tagore, one meant for Indian nationalism (Jana gana Mana Adhinayaka Jayahe) and the other for the Bengali sub-nationalism (Amar Sonar Bangle, Ami Tomay Bhalobasi)[59], became the national anthem of two countries. In the Hindi Heartland, not only the process of regional identity was absent, the concurrent process of capitalist transformation and concomitant edifice of incentive structure got stunted. Thus, in the Hindi Heartland, the emergence of sub-nationalism had been a much weaker process. The emergence of a sub-national identity in the Hindi Heartland was further obstructed by the fact that Hindi, as a language, was far from standardized. Between Bihar in the east and Rajasthan on the west, linguists have identified at least one dozen variants of the language, each one spoken by at least 20 million people. Consequently, the possibility of the linguistic identity which could lay the seeds for a regional social identity was also not there. In the context of literacy programmes, these two related phenomena the absence of strong regional identity and a middle class which has spearheaded the social movements in most other parts of the country meant that much of the Hindi Heartland is still guided by a value system which does not accord adequate recognition to education as a critical individual endowment. Thus, literacy is a far less 'felt' need of the illiterate here. In many other parts of India, this element of modernisation (which made people conscious of the fact that education is a universal necessity and it should not to be confined to a small elite only) was the outcome of the social movements that had taken place in late nineteenth or early twentieth century. These areas have responded more positively to the development programmes that were started in the post-independence era, including the literacy programmes.

Development Experience in Hindi Heartland

The states of the Hindi Heartland pose the toughest developmental challenge for India. These states are considered laggard and a blot in the overall profile of India which has experienced at least some progress in recent decades and considerably integrated itself with the international economic grid. The developmental bottlenecks in the Hindi Heartland are considered by many as a drain on the national exchequer, leading to counter divisive force, for "cessation of the successful". The successful states in south, west and north India feel disadvantaged that, in spite of their good track record in the developmental front, the successive Finance Commissions have penalized them in the matter of awarding the non-plan grant in the name of equalization. The feeling is not altogether unjustified. The talisman of "underdevelopment", they argue, seems to be a "boon" rather than "bane" for those poor states which are mainly located in the Hindi Heartland.

The success for a state, in the wake of liberalization, critically depends on its ability to attract investment. On this parameter, two categories of "states" have emerged in India since the liberalization. The first category consists of states that are reform-driven with an eye for the national and international market. A social class, not necessarily dependent on any individual charismatic leader, scripts this provincial agenda; they often have several in-house developmental icons. The agenda of this social class is further reinforced by a strong sub-national consolidation which inculcates a sense of provincial ownership. This instills not only a focused approach, but a very broad social consensus regarding the development strategy. In spite of their intense political differences, hardly any acrimony exists among the political parties in these states over the accepted provincial developmental agenda. The second category of states, mainly located in the Hindi Heartland, on the other hand, are still carrying the historical baggage of oppression by the British which included the extermination of their indigenous artisans, traders and entrepreneurs, and the archaic land tenure system that meant the absence of an incentive structure which could contribute to production and productivity, leading to accumulation. The draconian feudal legacy still stands in the way for the emergence of a development oriented middle class in these states. This had a far reaching consequence in the matter of quality of their governance. In most of these states, there were non-functioning governments, leading to domination of either the "mafia" or the "radical forces" which operate outside the constitutional structure of the country. To a great extent, the mafia or the radical outfits do social mediation, apart from pursuing their own agenda. Now, several districts of the Hindi Heartland are operationally outside the formal governmental authority. In this overall scenario of near social stagnation in the Hindi Heartland states, Uttar Pradesh and Bihar, however, had unfolded a new brand of social leadership leading to the establishment of their electoral hegemony. This was not the case in most of the developed states where, whatever may be the political complexion of different ruling parties; their social base remained essentially the same. They, thus, had long experience of running the governmental apparatus with élan, confidence and efficiency. In Bihar and Uttar Pradesh, however, there emerged new ruling elites because of democratization. The transition took places first from 'traditional' to 'vernacular' elites; later, thanks to further democratization, from 'vernacular' to 'cockney' elites. The social base of cockney elites is such that they are either outside or on the fringe of the 'market'. Their discourse is not routed around the Euro- centric model, which guided the traditional elite and to a lesser extent even the 'vernacular' elite. So when the market-centric strategy was ushered in India after liberalisation, they had no clue about the possible development agenda, other than the state's role as a 'provider'. Such an understanding of state has obvious limitations vis-à-vis its developmental role. A state cannot go far in the realm of development and social justice, without a functioning and well-oiled state structure. The strengthening of the state structure, in turn, depends on the availability of public finance. With the plummeting of national growth, there is a possibility of substantial decline in the collection of revenue. This will affect the Hindi Heartland states far more than the other ones. However, since 2004, with the increase in the Tax/ GDP ratio, the devolution of the Finance Commission to the states has increased manifold, which in turn displayed higher growth rate for the Hindi- Heartland states, particularly Bihar.

In the last sixty years, the process of building of the state structure was nearly complete in most regions of the country and at the centre. The first task in this process was value addition to the inherited colonial administration, apart from reinventing the chain of command for the development administration, parallel to the general administration. Over and above, it also entailed administrative reform and creation of new institutions to serve the development agenda. Such strengthening of the state and the consequent economic development lead to a growing market. Later, this growing market takes care of the development needs, even when the "state" opts to retreat. In this context, one should understand that the shifting of Tata's NANO plant from West Bengal to Gujarat indicated the generic strength of the former "ryatwari settled" state along with its vibrant market. In the process, Gujarat could attract a large investment with better incentive. This is not so much due to the negotiating skill of Narendra Modi, the then Chief Minister, but the triumph of the financially powerful provincial state structure of Gujarat, that was assiduously built by its successive Chief Ministers.

Nevertheless, all components of state building were not uniformly achieved even in the successful provinces. Nehru became the national icon of state building effort, because he did not script it on basis of techno-managerial thrust alone, but added to it the politics of inclusion and ideology. This model of state building was followed by several provinces in the south by K. Kamraj, in the north by Pratap Singh Kairon, in the west by Y.B. Chavan, and in the east by Biju Patnaik. The provinces which built new state structures in the early years after independence are now in the forefront of development. Unfortunately, in the Hindi Heartland states, the agenda of state building was never taken up. Bihar, a "permanent settlement" region, was ruled by intermediaries under the nomenclature of Zamindars and the state building effort was stunted here by the limited revenue generation by successive governments. The absence of a development vision of various post-independence regimes further stunted the evolution of the state structure here.[60]

It is extremely ironic that, in spite of being a failed state, the process of electoral democratization in Bihar had continued unabated, under the spell of socialist, communist, radical and social justice movements. This has resulted into a complete change in political power structure. But unfortunately, with wider democratization in the polity, there was also a commensurate process of collapse of the state structure. Indeed, the elites of all complexions, from "traditional" to "cockney", were never preoccupied with the important agenda of building of an efficient state structure. The traditional elite felt that an enabled state structure would continue the institutional reform beyond the Zamindari abolition, threatening not only their feudal interest but also ultimately their political hegemony. In contrast, the cockney elite who dethroned the traditional elite, could not understand the importance of the instruments of state for an inclusive development process. The social base of cockney elite being outside the market structure and their production being generally wedded to self-consumption, they could not realise the importance of a facilitating state to provide critical agricultural inputs like seed, fertiliser and irrigation. In the process, not only economic development continued to lag behind, but even the power structure in the lower levels could not be broken. Under such circumstance, whatever limited authority the state structure had in Bihar had become even more limited. Fortunately, after 2005, the Bihar brand of "coalition of extreme" had not only restored the authority of the state and ensured dramatic growth, but had also broken the lower centres (PRI's) of power by positive discrimination in favour of the marginals, women and Dalit. The above "coalition" was broken in 2013, with the counter "coalition of poor and inarticulate". This coalition has been further expanded, after the parliamentary election of 2014.[61]

In two other Hindi Heartland states, Madhya Pradesh and Rajasthan, even though the state structure was not very powerful, it had to compete with a relatively better track record of the "Princely" estates in those states in terms of governance. The continued hold of the scions of the Princely estates in the post-independence politics of Madhya Pradesh and Rajasthan can only be understood in terms of the developmental role they have played historically in their respective regions. Historically speaking, they were fulcrums of some moderate industrialization in some parts of the region. The incentive structure there was embedded in the ownership of the respective domains. Unlike the landlords of the "Permanent Settlement" areas who were only interested in collection of rents, they (the Princes) had full sense of ownership of their respective principalities. This, in turn, had implied an inbuilt incentive structure for development. Parallel to the efforts of industrialization by Mysore, Travancore-Cochin and Gaekwad states, the Scindias of Gwalior or Holkars of Indore, two mega principalities of Madhya Pradesh, also set up state enterprises and helped Indian capitalists to establish factories within their territories. The political separateness of the native states from British India was more important for industrial growth, largely compensating for the semi-feudal structure of administration of those states, given the discrimination practiced against Indian businessmen under the imperial system.Even the Princely estate of Bhopal played a decisive role in modernization and urbanization of the area. Bhopal was not only known as Baghdad of India because of its rich Muslim culture, its tradition of tolerance and the progressive nature of its institutions had also ensured its distinguished place in the country's overall social scenario. Thus, after independence, Bhopal was chosen the capital of the sprawling state of Madhya Pradesh. Incidentally, most of the economically developed and better-governed regions of Madhya Pradesh were earlier Princely estates, not from the areas under the tutelage of British India. Thus, in spite of feudal structure and the absence of even a modicum of democracy, the Princes were generally not object of derision or revulsion in Madhya Pradesh, as Zamindars were in Bihar. It was not surprising that after the introduction of the parliamentary democracy, Princes in Madhya Pradesh and Rajasthan could win many elections; in contrast, most of the Zamindars in the Bihar plain were routed in the elections whenever they opted for it.[62] Similarly, even though Wazid Ali Shah was dethroned, immediately after the First War of Independence, he continued to have powerful impact on the urban culture of Uttar Pradesh.[63] In the post-independence period, when most of the Princely estates got unilaterally annexed to India, they were generally ruled by the Congress party. But later, because of several policies of the Congress government, including abolition of Privy Purses, the Princes got gradually alienated from the Congress Party. Initially, they trekked to the Swantantra Party, led by C. Rajagopalachari, and later to Jan Sangh, now the Bhartiya Jan Party.

Conclusion

The "Idea of the Hindi Heartland" in some sense is self-explanatory. But Hindi, the language lubricant, which had constructed the cultural identity of the region, was "ill-positioned to be sympathetic to the anti- Brahminical critique that was gathering strength elsewhere".[64] This was particularly related to the "emergent Brahmin of the post-1857 Hindi Heartland".[65] This got further reinforced with the artificial divide between Hindi and Urdu, even though both the languages had common ancestry. Over the years, "Urdu" got associated with "Muslims" and "Hindi" with "Hindus". "The shared history of Hindi-Urdu's evolution (and subsequent division) is sought to be denied by the competing purist on the either side, who seek to blame each other for the process of linguistic division that both admit, at least implicitly, is culturally damaging".[66] Incidentally, on September 4, 2014, Supreme Court approved "Uttar Pradesh's 1989 legislation adopting Urdu as the second official language of the state. The ruling by a five-judge bench said laws of the country were not rigid, but accommodative to secure the linguistic secularism". The judgment came in response to "UP Hindi Sahitya Sammelan's appeal challenging the Uttar Pradesh Official Language (Amendment) Act. The SC referred to several states which have adopted other officially recognized languages in addition to Hindi".[67] The linguistic and cultural construct of the judgment of Supreme Court, was absolutely valid. Urdu is one of the pulsating cultural legacies of the Hindi Heartland, along with the "huge reservoir of Bhakti poetry which, in Braj and in Awadhi, in music …swept across practically the whole of India".[68] The Hindustani classical music is also part of this heritage. Interestingly, Union Minority Affairs Minister Najma Heptullah's statement that "anybody living in this country is a Hindu"[69] (later, however, she retracted from her statement and said that she used the word "Hindi", not "Hindu") will obviously be interpreted in two ways since she is a politician. But, the best idea would be to do away with the language-religion link. Hindi has never been a Hindu-only language, just as Urdu has never been an all- Muslim legacy.

Even though the social base of the sanskritised Hindi was limited, the hegemony of Benaras and the massive state patronage later, ensured the authority of Hindi. The Devanagari script was promoted by "the Hindi literary scholars of Benaras and used by those educated people of Bihar who had been influenced by the Benaras school".[70] Similarly, "Gurumukhi", a symbol of Sikh religious scriptures, which was not tied to a particular class or caste, became a reinforcing symbol of distinctiveness of Punjabi from the Hindi language. In contrast, the Maithili script, usually limited within the "Maithil" Brahmin and "Karna" Kayastha of Bihar, could not be associated with the mass culture of the region. In the process, Maithili could not be mass language of the people. Incidentally, Hindi is not the mother tongue of any of the major population group of Bihar. Two of the major ethnic groups, Magahi and Bhojpuri, in the absence of a "standard literary language of their own, chose to adopt Hindi as the medium of education".[71]

Early Hindi ideologues were not the only ones who detested any anti- Brahmin voice of the past centuries; even figures "like Kabir, and a tradition like Bhakti, had to wait for recognition by a later generation of "progressive" thinkers, before it could be assimmilated into and then become the glorious past of modern Hindi". Prem Chand, unlike many of his contemporaries wrote fearlessly and trenchantly against the Brahminical order. Unfortunately, his writings were not backed by something parallel like the anti-Brahmin Dravidian movement of south or movement by Phule or Sahuji Maharaj of Kolhapuri in old Bombay Presidency. Indeed, his writings invited venomous wrath of the Brahmins, because it tended to "generate loathing for Brahmins".[72]

One Jyoti Prasad Nirmal called him "ghrina ke pracharak"[73], that is the preacher of disgust. In one of his writings, Prem Chand further reinforces his 'brand' : "in three-fourths of my stories, I have shown my prejudice by painting Brahmins in dark colours... if I had enough strength, I would devote my whole life to freeing the Hindu community from the priests, the parasites who feed of religion. The greatest disgrace, the leprous scab of the Hindu community is precisely such petty groups, who are like gigantic leech, sucking away the life-blood of the community."[74] The liberation of the Hindi language from the Brahminical stranglehold and insularity was not only voiced by a litterateur, but by another resident of the great city of Allahabad, Pandit Jawaharlal Nehru. In his autobiography, nearly a century ago, he wrote "I criticized the intricate and ornate language that was customary in Hindi writing, full of difficult Sanskrit words, artificial, and clinging to ancient forms. I ventured to suggest that this courtly style addressed to a select audience, should be given up, and Hindi writers should deliberately write for the masses and in language understood by them. Mass contacts would give new life and sincerity to the language, and the writers themselves would catch emotional energy of the masses..."[75]. He further suggested that the cognitive world of the Hindi constituency should be enlarged, its authors should pay more attention to "Western thought and literature ... it would be desirable to have translations from the classics of the European languages as well as books dealing with modern ideas"[76]. He concluded that "modern Bengali, Gujarati and Marathi were little more advanced in these matters than modern Hindi, and certainly more creative work has been done in Bengali in recent years than in Hindi".[77] Like Prem Chand, Nehru was also severely criticized and he was called "ignoramus".[78] Thus, there was a parallel concerted effort in the Hindi Heartland to change its archaical "brand".

One may note here that the recent demise of U. R. Anathamurthy, spirited upholder of the cosmopolitan heritage of India, was hailed by the Bajrang Dal. His cosmopolitan construction was based on the cause of Kannada, the critique of the Brahminical social order, and the world view on which "he has been raised".[79] He was possibly the best example of self-loathing. So it is not a historical accident that not only the idea of Kannada sub-nationalism has been robust and strong, but Karnataka has been the bastion of one of the strongest knowledge industry in present India. Incidentally, the largest number of the recipients of the Jnan Peeth Awards in the post-independence period has been from Karnataka. If the Hindi Heartland society has to have a robust social anchor, it has to emulate the trajectory of Karnataka.

The suggested names for Bharat Ratna in the Times of India, of August 10, mentioned in the introductory part of my lecture, may not be negotiable. However, the benchmark achieved by the Gutenberg Press of Germany and Gita Press of Gorakhpur in printing and distribution of religious texts are unmatched. In some sense, Johaness Gutenberg[80] and Hanuman Prasad Poddar,[81] the founder of the Gita Press had similarities and convergence point in their respective career, even though separated by five centuries. Incidentally, Prime Minister Narendra Modi gifted Gita to the Emperor of Japan, in his current visit there.[82]

In the twentieth century in India, "Shivkasi" Calendar Art in the print media earlier and Ramanand Sagar, in the electronic media later, completely changed the fundamental aesthetics sensibilities. The "Ramayan" and the "Mahabharat" serials reinvented the psyche of the Indian in the most unprecedented manner. At the time of the relay or broadcast of the serials, the streets will be deserted and most of the people huddled before the television sets. The reach of the "Shivkasi" Calendar Art or the "Ramanand Sagar" centric television serials media, had far more influence in dissemination and reach of "Hindu" and "Celestial" identity, than what Gutenberg or Gita Press could have. Government of India should order two more medallions from the RBI mint, to be given to either Pratapnarayan Mishra and Ramanand Sagar, or to Rahul Sanskritayan and Ganesh Shankar Vidyarthi.

Hypothetically, the idea and the contour of the Hindi-Heartland will be determined on the basis of which of the two twins will get the Bharat Ratna. While the former extols the past, the latter is quintessentially self-loather. Let me end my contention with a quote from celebrated author Mike Marqusee's, on the therapeutic power of self-loathing. He opines that "anyone who entirely lacks this trait is not to be trusted. And it is generally acknowledged as an ethical principle that with corrections of the self comes the chastisement of others. For the privileged self, a form of self-rejection not personal, but political may be necessary to reach out to others, to know oneself, and become fully human'. Hindi Heartland has to co-opt and internalize the foundation of Mike Marqusee's of self loathing for placing itself on a path of comprehensive development economic, social, political and cultural. As an optimist, I hope this challenge will soon be taken up by the intelligentsia of the Hindi Heartland. identities: The interplay of gender, religion and politics in India. Eds. Leslie, Julia and McGee, Mary. New Delhi, Oxford University Press, 99-132.

References

1. '5 Bharat Ratna medallion from the RBI Mint', *The Times of India,* Patna Edition, August 10, 2014, p-15.
2. Ibid.
3. Ibid.
4. 'Prez honours 28 for contribution towards in Hindi', *The Times of India*, Patna Edition,August 28, 2014, p-7
5. 'Ninety days of the Modi Government Avision yet to Emerge' by S.L. Rao, *in The Telegraph,* Patna Edition, Patna, August 18, 2014, p-6.
6. Ibid.
7. Rai,Alok, 'How to make it difficult for the gabblers why not add another compulsory 'vernacular' language component to the CSAT?', *Indian Express*, Delhi Edition,August 8, 2014, p-15.
8. Ibid.
9. Shankar, Kalyani, 'Modi Completes the formality', *Millenium Post*, New Delhi,August 20, 2014, p-8.
10. Brass, Paul R., Language, *Religion & Politics in North India*, Cambridge University Press, USA 2005, p-71.
11. Yadav, Yogendra, 'And the winner is English', August 4, 2014, *indianexpress.com/article/opinion/columns/and-the-winner-is-english*
12. SABJANTA.NET
13. 'Hindi is an official Language', *the Telegraph*, Calcutta, p-1, April 20, 2013.
14. Mallikarjun, B, 'Fifty Years of Language for Modern Hindi : The Official Language of India', *in Language in India*, www.languageindia.com.
15. Grierson, G.A, *Linguistic Survey of India*, 1901, Vol. VI.
16. Ibid.
17. Mallikarjun, B, op.cit
18. Mallikarjun, B, op.cit
19. Mallikarjun, B, op.cit.
20. Mallikarjun, B, op.cit.
21. Premchand, one of the most celebrated writers of the Indian subcontinent, is regarded as one of the foremost Hindustani writers of early twentieth century.
22. 'Renu' is placed amongst the pioneering Hindi writers, who brought peripheral voices into the mainstream of Hindi literature.
23. Suryakant Tripathi 'Nirala' pioneered Chhayavad. Parimal and Anaamika are considered as original Chhayavaadi Hindi literature.
24. Firaq was writer, critic, and according to one commentator, one of the most noted Urdu poets of India. His original name was Raghupati Sahay.
25. Nagarjun was major Hindi & Maithili poet. He penned a number of novels, short stories, literacy biographies and travelogues, He was known as Janakavi the people's poet.
26. Mahadevi Verma was best known as an outstanding Hindi poet, and was a freedom fighter, women's activist and educationist from India.

27. Hazari Prasad Dwivedi was a Hindi novelist, literary historian and scholar. He did research on medieval religious movement of India, specially Kabir and 'Nath Sampradaya'.
28. Ramavriksha 'Benipuri' was a reputed writer in Hindi. He was also a journalist of repute. He was associated with the socialist movement.
29. Ram Vilas Sharma was an eminent progressive literary critic, linguist, poet and thinker. He was wedded to Marxism.
30. Harishankar 'Parsai' was a noted satirist and humorist of modern 'Hindi' literature. He is known for his simple and direct style.
31. Sharad Joshi was Hindi poet, writer, satirist and a dialogue & script writer in Hindi films and television.
32. Krishna Chander was a prolific writer. He wrote mainly in 'Urdu', but was well-versed in Hindi & English.
33. Yashpal was a Hindi-language author who often considered to be the most-gifted since Premchand.Apolitical commentator and a socialist, who had a particular concern for the welfare of the poor and the disadvantaged.
34. Mahapandit Rahul Sankrityayan was called the Father of Hindi Travel literature. He was a multilingual linguist, and well versed in several languages and their dialects.
35. Ganesh Shankar Vidyarthi was an outstanding journalist, wedded to the cause of poor and marginals. In March 1931, commercial riots flared up in Kanpur. Vidyarthi tried his best to restore communal peace and harmony, but was killed in an affected
36. Dalmia, Vasudha, *The Nationalisation of Hindu Traditions : Bharatendu Harischandra and Nineteenth-century Banaras,* Oxford University Press, Delhi, 1997, p-28.
37. Ibid.
38. Francesca Orsini, *The Hindi Public Sphere 1920-1940 Language and Literature in the Age of Nationalism*, Oxford University Press, New Delhi, 2002.
39. Ibid p-111.
40. Dalmia, Vasudha, op.cit. p-27.
41. Dalmia, Vasudha, op.cit. p-27.
42. Gupta, Shaibal, "A messiah for Bihar", Seminar, 480,August 1999, p-38.
43. Dalmia, Vasudha, op.cit. p-94.
44. Dalmia, Vasudha, op.cit. p-94.
45. Dalmia, Vasudha, op.cit. p-97.
46. Dalmia, Vasudha, op.cit. p-95.
47. Dalmia, Vasudha, op.cit. p-64.
48. Dalmia, Vasudha, op.cit. p-64.
49. Dalmia, Vasudha, op.cit. p-64.
50. Dalmia, Vasudha op.cit. p-64.
51. Dalmia, Vasudha, op.cit. p-85.
52. Dalmia, Vasudha, op.cit, pp-85/86.
53. Dalmia, Vasudha, op.cit. p-94.
54. 'Kyoto, Varanasi to turn partner city affiliates', *in Sunday Hindustan Times*, Patna Edition, August 31, 2014, p-6.

55. Ibid.
56. 'RSS bid to woo Dalits', *The Telegraph*, Patna Edition, September 7, 2014, p-7.
57. Ibid.
58. Ibid.
59. Gupta, Shaibal, *Idea of Bihar : ALecture*, Monograph 02/2013, ADRI, Patna, p-10.
60. Lall, Sunita & Gupta, Shaibal, 'Introduction' in *Resurrection of the State : A Saga of Bihar Essays in Memory of Papiya Ghosh*, Manak Publication Pvt. Ltd., New Delhi-2013, p-xvi.
61. Ibid, p-xvii.
62. Ibid, p-xviii.
63. Gupta, Shaibal, 'Idea of Bihar :ALecturer', op.cit. p-15.
64. Rai,Alok, 'Some Reflections on the Premchand Dalit Controversy', p-157.
65. Ibid.
66. Rai, Alok, 'Longing for Urdu', p-281.
67. 'SC puts stamp on Urdu as 2nd language of UP', *The Hindustan Times*, Patna Edition, September 05, 2014, p-9.
68. Rai, Alok, 'Longing for Urdu', p-277.
69. 'Nothing wrong in calling all Indians 'Hindu' Najma' in *the Hindustan Times*, Patna Edition,August 29, 2014, p-1.
70. Brass, Paul, op.cit. p-67.
71. Brass, Paul, op.cit. p-69.
72. Rai, Alok, 'Some Reflections on the Premchand Dalit Controversy', p-161.
73. Ibid, p-161.
74. Ibid, p-161.
75. Nehru, Jawaharlal, 'An Autobiography', Penguin Books, India, New Delhi, 2014, p-473
76. Ibid, p-474.
77. Ibid, p-474.
78. Ibid, p-474.
79. Kesavan, Mukul, 'U.R. Ananthamurthy' 1932-2014 Fully human, *The Telegraph*, Patna Edition, August 25, 2014, p-6.
80. In 1436, Johaness Gutenberg, a German Goldsmith, began designing a machine capable of producing pages of text at in incredible speed. Gutenberg initiated the printing revolution, which brought about, Renaissance, Reformation, the age of Enlightenment and Scientific revolution. Gutenberg Bible (also known as 42-line Bible) has been acclaimed for its high aesthetic and technical quality. Gutenberg Press was responsible for the larger circulation of Bible.
81. Hanuman Prasad Poddar (1892-1971) is the founder of Gita Press, Gorakhpur. The institution's main objective is to promote and spread the principles of Sanatana Dharma, the Hindu religion, among the general public by publishing Gita, Ramayana, Upanishads, Puranas, etc.
82. 'PM takes a dig at 'Secular' forces over gifting the Gita' in Hindustan Times, Patna Edition, September 3, 2014, p-7.

Cultures in Contact : Acculturation and Change

John W. Berry

Multiculturalism Policy in Canada

With this general orientation to how societies may deal with cultural diversity as background, we turn now to the question of how Canada treats these issues.

While numerous attempts were made historically to assimilate Canada's diverse population to British cultural norms (Palmer, 1975), by 1956 the Federal Government's view was that assimilation had not worked anywhere in the contemporary world, and that it was impracticable as a general policy. By 1971, largely in response to the Report of the Royal Commission on Bilingualism and Biculturalism (particularly to Book IV, "The Cultural Contributions of the Other Ethnic Groups"), the Prime Minister announced a policy of multiculturalism, the key elements of which were designed to achieve harmonious intercultural relations by promoting simultaneously *cultural maintenance*, by all cultural groups, and intergroup *contact and participation* in the larger society:

> "National unity, if it is to mean anything in the deeply personal sense, must be founded on confidence in one's own individual identity; out of this can grow respect for that others and a willingness to share ideas, attitudes and assumptions. A vigorous policy of

Cultures in Contact : Acculturation and Change, 21st-22nd February, 1997
G.B. Pant Social Science Institute

multiculturalism will help create this initial confidence. It can form the base of a society which is based on fair play for all.... The government will support and encourage the various cultures and ethnic groups that give structure and vitality to our society. They will be encouraged to share their cultural expression and values with other Canadians and so contribute to a richer life for all." (Government of Canada, 1971, p. 3-4).

To assist our understanding of this policy, we may identify and place four elements of the policy in a framework (see Figure 1) which also displays a number of their inter-relationships (see Berry, 1984a). First, the policy wishes to avoid assimilation by encouraging ethnic groups to maintain and develop themselves as distinctive groups within Canadian society; this element we term "own group maintenance and development". Second, a fundamental purpose of the policy is to increase intergroup harmony and the mutual acceptance of all groups which maintain and develop themselves; this we term "other group acceptance and tolerance". Third, the policy argues that own group development by itself is not sufficient to lead to other group acceptance; "intergroup contact and sharing" is also required. Fourth, full participation by groups cannot be achieved if some common mode of communication is not learned; thus the "learning of official languages" is also encouraged by the policy. In addition to identifying these four elements of the policy, Figure 1. also displays some inter-relationships (connecting lines between elements). A few of these are explicit in the policy, others are implicit, and others will be referred to in this paper, when considering the social-psychological literature on ethnic relations.

A central question is whether the policy intends to encourage the maintenance of numerous and full-scale cultural systems (as implied in the term multi-*culturalism*), or whether it is designed to be supportive of some lesser phenomenon (such as various aspects of *ethnicity* which are derived from a full cultural system). Burnet (1975) has argued that "ethnicity" rather than "culture" is the actual and realistic focus of such a policy: most groups lack their own separate social and political institutions, many lack their own (ancestral) language and their numbers are not always large. Thus the

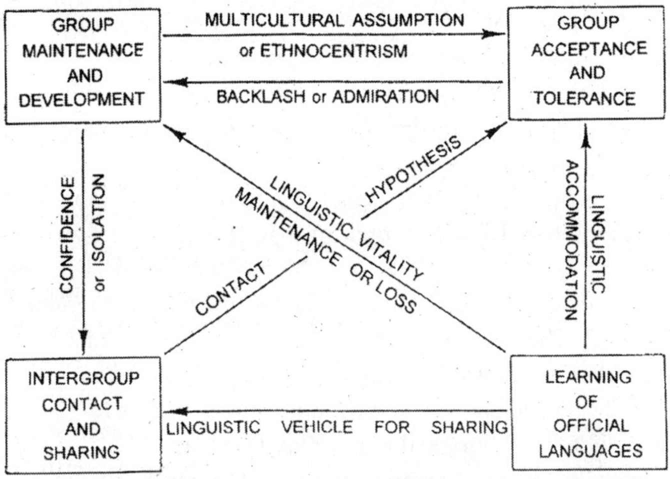

Fig. 1 : Four Components of 1971 Multiculturalism Policy
(Source : Berry, 1984a)

maintenance of shared features which are derived from a heritage culture (i.e. ethnic phenomena) are more likely to be possible than the maintenance of full-scale cultures ("museum cultures" in Burnet's, 1975, terms).

A second criticism has been levelled by John Porter (1972, 1975), who argued that maintaining an interest in ethnicity merely perpetuates ethnic stratification in Canadian society: multiculturalism may serve only to keep particular groups in their place in the "vertical mosaic". It may also provide a basis for discrimination (Lupul, 1989). While undoubtedly there has been important stratification according to ethnic group membership in the past, and perhaps at the present time for some groups, recent evidence (e.g., Boyd et al., 1981; Pineo and Porter, 1985; Breton et al., 1990) suggests that ethnicity is no longer a substantial predictor of status in Canada. Indeed, educational and occupational aspirations and attainments of some newer immigrant groups now exceed those of groups at the top of Porter's original hierarchy (Richmond, 1988; Samuda et al., 1989).

A third difficulty is that multiculturalism is widely viewed as a policy only for the non-British, non-French portions of the Canadian population. While having its roots in concerns expressed about the place of "the other ethnic groups", the initial policy statement in 1971, as well as more recent statements (see 1988/1989 Annual Report of the Ministry of Multiculturalism) emphasize that the policy is for *all* Canadians, dominant as well as non-dominant, majority as well as minority.

After a decade and a half with programmes based upon the 1971 statement, official multiculturalism was formally achieved by the enactment (on July 21, 1988) of a Multiculturalism Policy, entitled "An Act for the preservation and enhancement of multiculturalism in Canada". The Act is explicitly linked to a number of extant features of Canadian policy: the constitutional recognition of the importance of preserving and enhancing the multicultural heritage of Canadians, of the rights of Aboriginal peoples of Canada, and of two official languages in Canada; the equality of all Canadians, whether so by birth or by choice; the equality of opportunity, regardless of race, national or ethnic origin or colour; freedom from discrimination based on culture, religion or language; and the recognition of the diversity of Canadians as a fundamental characteristic of Canadian society. The specific clauses of the Act refer to a number of themes. Foremost among them are:

(1) the promotion of the freedom of all Canadians to "preserve, enhance and share their cultural heritage";
(2) the promotion of multiculturalism as "a fundamental characteristic of Canadian heritage and identity", and as an "invaluable resource in the shaping of Canada's future";
(3) the promotion of "full and equitable participation of individuals and communities of all origins", and the "elimination of barriers to such participation";
(4) the recognition of the contribution of Canadian cultural communities, and to "enhance their development";
(5) ensuring "individuals equal protection under the law, while respecting and valuing their diversity"; and
(6) encouraging Canadian institutions to be "both respectful and inclusive of Canada's multicultural character".

Other themes emphasize the creativity, and evolution that result from cultures in contact, and the importance of both heritage and official languages in Canada.

The 1989 "New Directions" of the Ministry of Multiculturalism (rooted in the new Act) retained many of these features, while giving new emphasis to certain aspects. The first new direction is "Race Relations and Cross-Cultural Understanding", and can be identified generally with the "tolerance" goal in the 1971 statement. However, the racial dimension is now at the fore, with public education, cross-cultural training and community-based initiatives being seen as the vehicles for pursuing a reduction in racial intolerance. The second new direction is "Heritage Cultures and Languages", and is similar to the "group maintenance" goal of the 1971 statement; while continuing cultural support programmes, there is a renewed emphasis on heritage language learning. The third new direction is "Community Support and Participation", and is related to the "contact and sharing" goal of the 1971 statement; however, there is now much greater emphasis on full and equal access to participation by all Canadians in all aspects of Canadian society. A fourth new 'initiative' is a "Cross-Government Commitment", one in which the multicultural view of Canada is promoted not just in the Department of Multiculturalism and Citizenship, but is encouraged in all Federal Departments.

Current Canadian views about the multiculturalism policy are as diverse as the population itself (Bourhis, 1994; Kalin & Berry, 1994). Despite the emphasis on "sharing" in the 1971 statement and 1988 Act, many Canadians are voicing the idea that an emphasis on our ethnic differences, even as a quality that characterizes us as a nation, reduces our achievement of becoming "Canadian" (Bibby, 1990; Spicer, 1991; Bisoondath, 1994). In part, the naming of the new Department as "multiculturalism and *Citizenship*" was intended to signal a balance between the age old Canadian opposition between "unity and identity" (Frye, 1971). Moreover, there is not yet a wide understanding of the change in emphasis from the "cultural maintenance" aspects of the policy to the "race relations" and "participation" programmes. For example, Spicer (1991, p. 129) proposes that :

> "...Federal government funding for multiculturalism activities other than those serving immigrant orientation, reduction of racial discrimination, and promotion of equality, should be eliminated..."

> However, Spicer's recommended set of priorities is virtually identical to those in place since 1989. In a sense, the pendulum appears to be swinging away from a concern for particular heritages, toward a concern for national unity, away from a celebration of our numerous cultural identities, toward the promotion of an emerging Canadian identity.

This policy initiative, and accompanying programmes to implement it, remains an important part of managing cultural pluralism in Canada. The question of public support for the policy and programmes, and of some social psychological dimensions (including the assumption that a sense of security or confidence is a necessary condition for tolerance) will be discussed later (see section 6, on Empirical Evidence).

Immigration and the Changing Canadian Population

Canada has always been culturally plural as a society (1871 Census: 60% British; 31% French; 9% others, including Native Peoples) However, a considerable impetus has been given to multiculturalism by the increasingly diverse sources of immigration over the past century. Initially from Eastern Europe, then from Southern Europe and now increasingly from other than Europe, immigration can be said to have given rise to multiculturalism (Hawkins, 1972; Palmer, 1976).

At the present time (1996 Census) British and French origins still account for the majority of the national population (39% and 24%, respectively) but this varies widely by region. Among other than British and French origins (37%), German, Italian, Ukrainian, Dutch and Aboriginal origins are the most frequent (ranging from 6.5% to 2% for these groups). While still relatively small in total number in Canada (6%) visible minorities represent substantial elements of regional and urban populations (11% in B.C., 9% in Ontario; 17% in Toronto and Vancouver, 10% in Calgary), their immigration continues at a relatively high proportion (over 60% of over 200,000 immigrants in 1996). Despite these numerous changes and trends, the proportion of foreign born has tended to remain a fairly constant proportion (between 15 and 20%) of the total population since Confederation,

Future trends are difficult to predict, given the volatile political and economic situations at present in various parts of the world. Indeed the "Demographic Review" (1989), while engaging in population projections in a number of demographic categories, avoided such projections with respect to ethnic origin. However, one study carried out for the Review (Balakrishnan, 1988) did project ethnic populations for 25 major urban areas and concluded that visible minority groups will increase to 10.7% of urban populations by the year 2001. In the country as a whole, however, this predicted increase is less likely to occur, since the bulk of current immigrants settle in the major urban centres. Samuel (1988) has predicted a national proportion of visible minorities of between 8.7 and 9.6%.

Ethnic and Race Relations in Canada

In this and the following section, the two main areas of psychological work in culturally plural societies are introduced and reviewed: ethnic relations and acculturation. As noted earlier, the two areas have remained distinct to a large extent, but there are sufficient parallels to draw them together. First, both areas arise only in culturally-plural societies: Second, they share a concern for group contact and resultant change in some basic social and psychological phenomena. Third, there is a central role for affective states (attitudes and ideologies) that indicate what people think and what they feel *should* be the case. Fourth, there are some obvious behavioural outcomes for individuals (changes in their behaviours and identities, and acts of discrimination). And, fifth both lead to an outcome that ranges from being stressful and conflict-ridden through to an adaptation that accommodates the needs of people in contact, both newcomers and the established larger society.

How can social psychology contribute to an understanding of the issues before us? In social psychology, the focus is typically on *individuals*, but we also usually aggregate our data into social and demographic categories. This has allowed the investigation of these phenomena at both the individual and group levels of analysis. The guiding conceptual framework for much of this work has been *ethnocentrism* theory, which is useful at both of these levels of analysis. The concept refers to the universal tendency for *groups* to generally favour themselves (i.e. an "ingroup bias" to have a relative preference for ones own group over others), while allowing for the possibility that some groups will exhibit this relative preference more than others. It also refers to *individuals* who typically show an ingroup bias, while again allowing for individual differences in the extent of this preference; some individuals will be very ethnocentric, while others will be less so.

The fundamental question with which we are concerned is: Under what conditions can we all live together in a plural society. Among the many other answers (involving economic, political and human rights issues), some psychological preconditions can be suggested:

> First, there needs to be general support for multiculturalism, including acceptance of various aspects and consequences of the policy, and of cultural diversity as a valuable resource for a society. Second, there should be overall low levels of intolerance or prejudice in the population. Third, there should be generally positive mutual attitudes among the various ethnocultural groups that constitute the society. And fourth, there needs to be a degree of attachment to the larger Canadian society, but without derogation of its constituent ethnocultural groups. (Berry & Kalin, 1995, p. 302)

The study of ethnic and race relations is a vast topic, one that cannot possibly be covered in this paper. To open the discussion, Figure 2 illustrates some current conceptualizations. Results of empirical studies will be presented later.

The Figure can be looked upon as a "map" of relationships between some social and cultural factors (at the top), and the main psychological variables (in the lower box) used in the psychological study of ethnic and race relations. Three kinds of psychological variables are identified : cognition (involving the processes of perception and categorization of people and the attribution of characteristics to them); evaluation (involving judgements about their acceptance or rejection); and overt behaviour or action on the part of the individual (involving acts of discrimination against them).

There is considered to be a sequence to these psychological

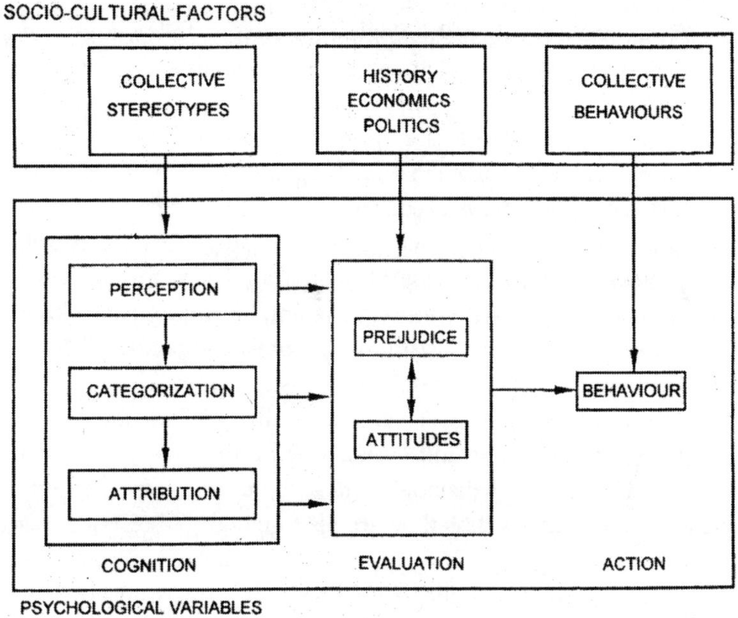

Fig. 2 : Framework for Examining Relationships between Socio-cultural and Psychological Factors in Research on Ethnic Group Relations

activities, beginning with the perception of similarities and differences among individuals in a population (e.g., tallness/ shortness; long hair/ short hair; light skin/dark skin etc). This is followed by a cognitive categorization of individuals into groups based on perceived patterns of similarities and differences (e.g., ales/females; blacks/whites etc). The act of categorization, by itself, is known (e.g., Tajfel, 1978) to have two consequences: the exaggeration of perceived similarity within categories, and of perceived difference between categories. Third, psychological characteristics are attributed by the perceiver to individual members of the categories; because of the effects of categorization noted above, this attribution tends to overgeneralize the similarity of characteristics within, and the difference between, the groups. This whole sequence while rooted in these three fundamental psychological processes, is also guided by collective images that have been generally shared in the sociocultural context, probably for many generations.

A second set of psychological processes follows, involving the making of value judgements and the exhibiting of personal preferences. When these are linked to a specific group, the concept of ethnic *attitude* is employed; these can be favourable or unfavourable. However, when there is a generalized value judgement, the concept of *prejudice* is used; this is typically a negative or hostile evaluation, although in principle, positive prejudices are possible. The development and holding of such attitudes and prejudices are rooted in an individual's emotional system, but they are also known to be linked to numerous historical, economic and political factors in the sociocultural system in which one has grown up.

The third psychological variable is that of individual action, in which the cognitions and evaluations of the individual become expressed in actual behaviour. These behaviours are subject to personal motivations, but they are also guided (either encouraged or suppressed) by shared norms in society, such as laws, or social movements. It is important to note that individuals do not always express their cognitions and evaluations about ethnic and racial groups in overt ways; hence, psychologists have had to develop measurement techniques to dig more deeply and indirectly into the phenomena of stereotypes, prejudice and attitudes.

Because ethnic groups tend to vary on a number of dimensions, psychologists have attended to these possible confounds. Such dimensions as culture, race, religion and language are known to interact in complex ways; hence they require independent conceptualization and measurement. For example, an immigrant from India may be admired or rejected on the basis of cultural values, racial features, religion or accent; we would not know the extent of influence of each factor on a person's attitude unless we first made the distinction, and then attempted independent assessment of each factor. This possible "multiple causation" of behaviour makes it difficult to know, for any particular study group or individual, which factor is responsible, or which factors in combination lie at the root of discrimination or conflict.

Of course, no programme to understand or improve ethnic and race relations can attend only to these psychological phenomena. Clearly all the non-psychological factors identified at the top of

Figure 5 need to be attended to as well. Among these are four current issues in the social psychology of ethnic and race relations that have been prominent in the literature on multiculturalism in Canada: the institutional and normative nature of prejudice; the effects of security; the role of contact; and the importance of group similarity.

Prejudice. While prejudice is essentially a psychological phenomenon, it can become established in social norms and societal practices that may or may not any longer have negative effect or animosity underlying the practice (Duckitt, 1992). Hence a distinction has been drawn between personal and *institutional* prejudice. The former involves negative feelings by a person towards another person or group, while the latter may not; institutional prejudice is prejudice that has become conventional, but not necessarily with any personal intent to harm, injure or attack. Because of the different character of these forms of prejudice, change or control programmes would need to be different depending on whether one, the other (or both) of these are present.

Similarly, a distinction has been drawn between blatant and subtle prejudice. The former (sometimes called "old fashioned" prejudice) is revealed in overt acts of verbal or physical hostility (such as insults, attacks and deliberate acts of discrimination). The latter is covert (sometimes called "symbolic prejudice") and is revealed in "more acceptable" activities such as being opposed to various forms of equity or other social change programmes. In the last decade, changing social norms (both informal, and formal laws) have made blatant prejudice socially unacceptable, even illegal. Hence the expression of prejudice has become subjected to normative influence (as in the case of institutional prejudice) and can no longer be considered a purely psychological phenomenon.

Security. The 1971 Multiculturalism policy statement proposed that confidence in one's own individual identity was a plausible precondition for accepting the different identities of others. We have previously referred to this as the "multiculturalism assumption" (Berry, Kalin & Taylor, 1977), and this notion was included in Figure 4 as one possible relationship between "own group maintenance" and "other group tolerance". The assumption is that if one feels secure, and that one has a place in the Canadian mosaic, then one can be open and accepting also of a place for those who belong to other groups. Conversely, if ones identity is threatened or challenged, then one may not be in a position to be tolerant of others. The alternative relationship is also possible. that developing one's own group's confidence can lead to ethnocentrism (this also is illustrated in Figure 1). This alternative relationship is indeed the basis of ethnocentrism theory (LeVine & Campbell, 1972) in which positive own group attitudes are often negatively correlated with attitudes toward other groups.

Contact. Ever since the classic analyses of Amir (1976), it has been established that personal experience with members of other groups can lead to either increased liking or increased hostility; the outcome depends on some specific factors. Positive outcomes are likely when: there is equal status of the groups; the presence of common goals; and when contact is voluntary and intimate. Negative outcomes are likely when there is: status inequality; competition for scarce resources; and enforced interaction. When social conditions vary, the outcome of contact will vary; hence, attitude change is a social as well as a psychological phenomenon. Issues such as the "integrative capacity" of Canada to accept visible minority immigrants, and the possibility of a numerical "threshold" for such acceptance, are clearly related to the relationship between contact and prejudice. This relationship was also illustrated in Figure 1.

Group Similarity. An important element in intergroup and interpersonal attitudes is that of the similarity of the groups or persons in contact: it is well-established that the greater the similarity, then the greater the attraction. Whether found in experimental or in field studies, this relationship appears to be robust. It appears to apply both to psychological similarity in the case of interpersonal attraction (e.g., similar beliefs or interests are associated with greater liking) and to cultural similarity in the case of intergroup attraction (e.g., shared group characteristics, such as language, religion, values, norms are associated with greater group acceptance). An obvious implication of this relationship is that since groups who are now arriving as immigrants in Canada are rather dissimilar from those already established in the country, less acceptance of them may be expected, at least initially. To the extent that these groups acculturate to the larger society by adopting some generally shared Canadian norms and values, then increased acceptance may result. We now turn to a consideration of such acculturation phenomena.

Immigrant Acculturation

How IMMIGRANTS and ethnic groups adapt and change over time to the larger Canadian society is an important aspect of group relations (See Berry, 1990a, 1997). As we noted earlier, there are important parallels between ethnic relations and acculturation as cultural and psychological phenomena, both resulting in the possibility of outcomes ranging from positive mutual adaptations through to stress and conflict. We have also seen that in Canada not all the adaptation and change are expected to come from those newly-arrived: official multiculturalism policy involves the promotion of some adaptation on the part of the larger society (referred to as "institutional change"). Thus, acculturation is, in principle, a two-way street.

Acculturation was first identified as a cultural level phenomenon by anthropologists (e.g., Redfield et al, 1936) who defined it as culture change resulting from contact between two autonomous cultural groups. Although in principle, change occurs in both groups, in practice, more change occurs in the non-dominant than in the dominant group.

Acculturation is also an individual-level phenomenon, requiring individual members of both the larger society and the various acculturating groups to engage in new behaviours, and to work out new forms of relationships in their daily lives. This idea was introduced by Graves (1967), who has proposed the notion of "psychological acculturation" to refer to these new behaviours and strategies. One of the findings of subsequent research in this area is that there are vast individual differences in how people attempt to deal with acculturative change (termed "acculturation strategies"). These strategies have three aspects: their preferences ("acculturation attitudes"; see Berry et al., 1989); how much change they actually undergo ("behavioral shifts"; see Berry, 1980a); and how much of a problem these changes are for them (the phenomenon of "acculturative stress"; see Berry et al., 1987).

In all plural societies, cultural groups and their individual members, in both the dominant and non-dominant groups, must deal with the issue of how to relate to each other. Strategies with respect to two major issues are usually worked out by groups and individuals in their daily encounters with each other. These issues are: cultural *maintenance* (to what extent are one's cultural identity and characteristics considered to be important, and their maintenance strived for); and *contact and participation* (to what extent should they become involved with other cultural groups, or remain primarily among themselves). It is evident that these issues are two of the components identified in the Canadian multiculturalism policy.

When these two underlying issues are considered simultaneously, a conceptual framework (Figure 3) is generated which posits four strategies of acculturation and intercultural relations. These two issues can be responded to on attitudinal dimensions, represented by bipolar arrows. For purposes of presentation, generally positive or negative ("yes" or "no" responses) to these issues are illustrated, and intersect to define four strategies. These strategies carry different names, depending on which group (the dominant or nondominant) is being considered. From the point of view of *nondominant* groups, when individuals do not wish to maintain their cultural identity and

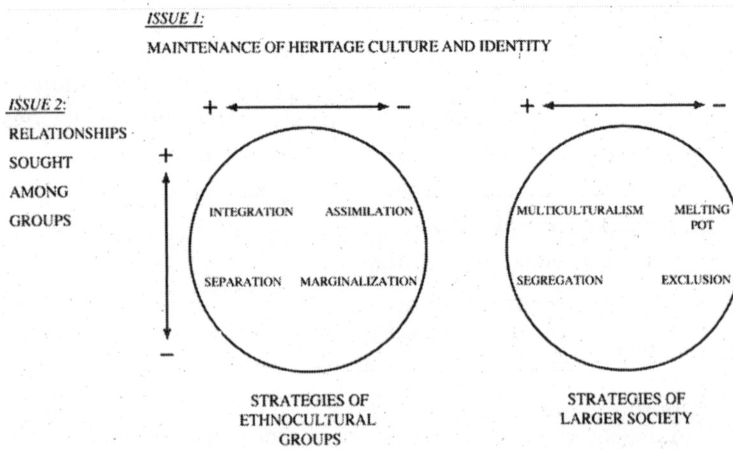

Fig. 3 : Acculturation strategies in ethnocultural groups and in the larger society

seek daily interaction with other cultures, the *Assimilation* strategy is defined. In contrast, when individuals place a value on holding onto their original culture, and at the same time wish to avoid interaction with others, then the Separation alternative is defined. When there is an interest in both maintaining one's original culture, while in daily interactions with other groups, *Integration* is the option; here, there is some degree of cultural integrity maintained, while at the same time seeking to participate as an integral part of the larger social network. Finally, when there is little possibility or interest in cultural maintenance (often for reasons of enforced cultural loss), and little interest in having relations with others (often for reasons of exclusion or discrimination) then *Marginalization* is defined.

This initial presentation was based on the assumption that non-dominant groups and their individual members have the freedom to choose how they want to acculturate. This, of course, is not always the case. When the dominant group enforces certain forms of acculturation, or constrains the choices of non-dominant groups or individuals, then other terms need to be used. The original anthropological definition clearly established that both groups in contact would change and become acculturated to each other. When we consider the views about how the dominant group in the larger society thinks that acculturation should take place, other terms are used (see right side of Figure 3). These have been termed acculturation expectations (Berry, 2003). Assimilation when expected by the dominant group is termed the Melting Pot. When Separation is forced by the dominant group it is Segregation. Marginalization, when imposed by the dominant group it is called Exclusion. Finally, Integration, when diversity is a widely accepted feature of the society as a whole, including by all the various ethnocultural groups, it is called Multiculturalism. In this definition, multiculturalism is not simply the continuing presence of many different cultural groups in a plural society, but also includes their equitable participation and inclusion in the larger society. These ways of acculturating, in both the non-dominant and dominant groups have been examined extensively in plural societies (Berry, 2017; Sam & Berry, 2016).

The view of acculturation and group relations illustrated in Figure 1. is clearly a *bi-dimensional* one. This conceptualization was introduced (Berry, 1970; Sommerlad & Berry, 1970) to challenge the *unidimensional* assumption that individuals can be viewed (and assessed) as being in a sort of "transition" between some "traditional" (or "minority") and some "modern" (or "mainstream") cultural situation. Ethnographic work among members of cultural communities generally reveals that their are two issues (cultural maintenance, and contact/participation), and that they are *independent* of each other. When the two dimensions are kept separate (both conceptually and empirically), the many varieties of acculturation become evident (Berry, 1980). Intercultural contact can lead to cultural homogeneity, to mixing or balancing, to rejection or to being rejected. The historical (and in much contemporary social psychology) bias is to assume that the "others" both want to, and will eventually, become like "us". Parallel conceptualization and research on cultural identity (Berry, 1970; Kalin & Berry, 1996; Ferdman, 1995; Phinney, 1990; Phinney et al, 1994) has shown that individuals are often comfortable with a bicultural identity; it is not necessary to choose one or the other in an inclusive, pluralistic society.

It is essential to note that the term *integration* as used here is not a euphemism for *assimilation*. Figure 3 clearly links Integration to a substantial degree of cultural maintenance (rather than to cultural loss or homogenization as in Assimilation). Just as importantly, it is evident that Integration can only be "freely" chosen and successfully pursued by nondominant groups when the dominant society is open and inclusive in their orientation toward cultural diversity (Berry, 1991). Thus, a *mutual accommodation* is required for Integration to be attained, involving the acceptance by everyone of the right of all groups to live together as culturally different peoples. This strategy requires nondominant groups to adopt the basic values of the larger society, while at the same time the dominant group must be prepared to adapt national institutions (e.g. education, health, labour) to better meet the needs of all groups now living together in the plural society.

Obviously, the integration strategy can only be pursued in societies that are explicitly *multicuitural* in which certain psychological pre-conditions are established (as described earlier, Berry & Kalin,

1995). These pre-conditions are::the widespread acceptance of the value to a society of cultural diversity (i.e. the presence of a positive "multicultural ideology"); relatively low levels of prejudice (i.e. minimal ethnocentrism, racism and discrimination); positive mutual attitudes among cultural groups (i.e. no specific intergroup hatreds); and a sense of attachment to, or identification with, the larger society by all groups (see also Kalin & Berry, in press).

Just as obviously, *integration* (and of course separation) can only be pursued when other members of ones ethnocultural group share in the wish to maintain the group's cultural heritage. In this sense, these two strategies are "collective", while *assimilation* is more "individualistic" (Moghaddam, 1988; Lalonde & Cameron, 1993).

Other terms than those used here have been proposed by researchers. In particular, the term "bicultural" has been employed to refer to acculturation that involves the individual simultaneously in the two cultures that are in contact (Szapocznik & Kurtines, 1993; La Fromboise et al, 1993; Cameron & Lalonde, 1994); this concept corresponds closely to the Integration strategy as defined here. Similarly, Gordon (1964) refers to two forms of incorporation: *cultural assimilation* and *structural assimilation.* In our terms, when both forms occur, complete assimilation is likely to result; however, when structural assimilation is present (a high degree of contact and participation) combined with a low degree of cultural assimilation (a high degree of cultural maintenance), then an outcome similar to Integration is likely.

Three other issues require commentary before proceeding, since preferences for one strategy over others are known to vary, depending on a number of variables. In measuring these strategies, a number of domains of daily behaviour (e.g., language, food, dress, club membership) are selected for which cultural choices can be made. For each domain, a statement is drafted for each of the four strategies; respondents indicate their preferences (usually on a 5-point scale) for each strategy. Despite there being diverse domains, there is usually an overall coherent preference for one particular strategy (as evidenced by Cronbach alpha coefficients in the .70 to .80 range; see Berry et al, 1989). However, there can be variation in relative preferences according to ones location: in more private spheres or domains (such as the home, the extended family, the cultural community) more cultural maintenance may be sought than in more public spheres (such as the work place, or in politics); and there may be less intergroup contact sought in private spheres than in the more public ones. Second, the broader national context may affect acculturation strategies, such that in explicitly multicultural societies individuals may seek to match such a policy with a personal preference for Integration; or in assimilationist societies, acculturation may be easiest by adopting an Assimilation strategy for oneself (Krishnan & Berry, 1992). That is, individuals may well be constrained in their choice of strategy, even to the point where there is a very limited role for personal preference. Indeed, when personal preferences are in conflict with national policies, stress may well result (Horenczyk, 1996). Third, there is evidence that during the course of development, and over the period of major acculturation, individuals explore various strategies, eventually settling on one that is more useful and satisfying than the others (Kim, 1988). However, as far as is known, there is no set sequence with which different strategies are used (Ho, 1995), nor specific ages at which one strategy is more likely to be used.

Both individuals and groups may exhibit various orientations toward their intercultural relations. These orientations consist of both preferences (*attitudes*) and actions (*behaviours*). Together, these attitudes and behaviours comprise what we have called *acculturation strategies* (Berry, 1990a). Attitudes towards these four alternatives have been measured in numerous studies (reviewed in Berry et al 1989). National policies and programmes may also be analysed in terms of these four approaches: some societies seek *assimilation*, expecting all ethnocultural groups to become like those in the dominant society; others seek *integration*, willing (even pleased) to accept and incorporate all groups to a large extent on their own cultural terms; yet others have pursued segregation policies; and others have sought the *marginalization* of unwanted groups. Thus the framework in Figure 6 can be used to analyse and categorize orientations toward cultural group relations of both individuals and groups in both the dominant and nondominant sections of society, and at three levels. These are illustrated in Figure 4.

LEVELS	DOMINANT	NON-DOMINANT
	• Mainstream • Larger Society	• Minority Group • Cultural Group
NATIONAL	National Policies	Group Goals
INDIVIDUAL	Multicultural Ideology	Acculturation Strategies
INSTITUTIONAL	Uniform or Plural	Diversity and Equity

Fig. 4 : Levels of Analysis and Use of Four Orientations

Inconsistencies and conflicts between these various acculturation strategies are one of many sources of difficulty for acculturating individuals. Generally, when acculturation experiences cause problems for acculturating individuals, we observe the phenomenon of *acculturative* stress (See Figure 5). In a recent overview of this area of research (Berry, 1997), it was argued that stress may arise, but it is not inevitable. Or as Beiser et al. (1988) have phrased it: migrant status is a mental health risk factor; but risk is not destiny.

On the left are shown group- or cultural-level phenomena, which are mainly *situational* variables; while to the right are individual- or psychological-level phenomena which are predominantly *person* variables. Along the top are features that exist prior to acculturation taking place, while along the bottom are those that arise during the process of acculturation. Through the middle of the framework are the main group and psychological acculturation phenomena; these flow from left to right beginning with the cultural groups in contact bringing about changes in many of their collective features (e.g., political, economic, social structures), then affecting the individual who is experiencing acculturation (resulting in a number of possible psychological experiences and changes, leading finally to a person's adaptation. The framework in Figure 5 combines both *structural* and *process* features: the central portion flowing from group acculturation through individual acculturation to adaptation is clearly a process taking place over time; factors in the upper and

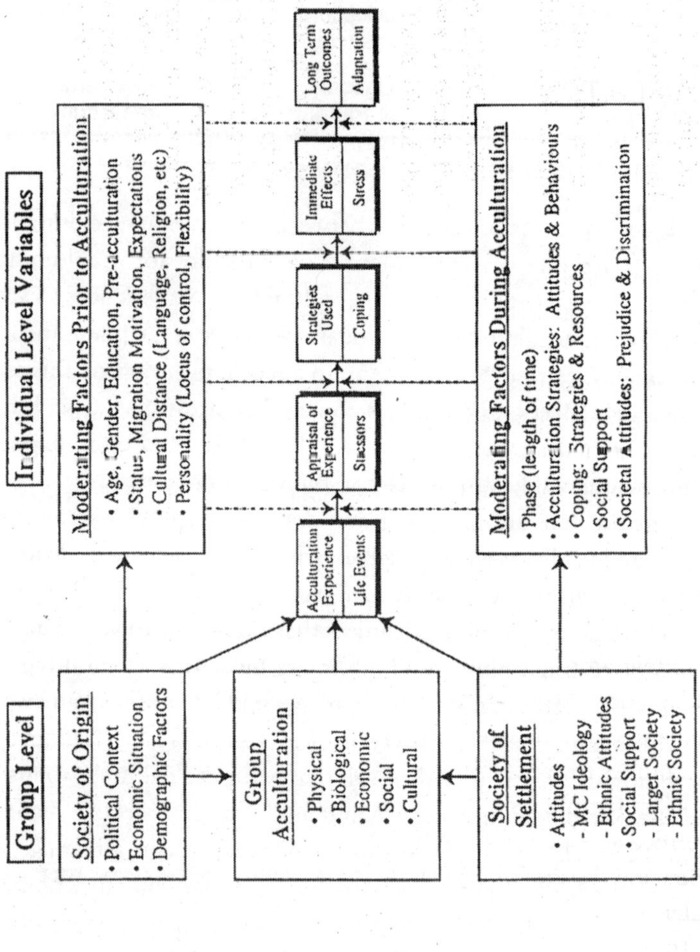

Fig. 5 : Factors Affecting Acculturative Stress

lower levels influencing this process provide the broad structure in which acculturation takes place.

Contemporary reviews of the literature (Berry & Sam, 1997; Ward, 1996) show that this central flow is highly variable: the nature of a person's psychological acculturation and eventual adaptation depends on specific features of the group-level factors (on the left) and of the moderating influence (shown by the dotted lines) of individual factors that exist prior to, or arise during, acculturation (at the top and bottom).

With respect to the structuring of. relationships, the model includes both *mediating* and *moderating* variables (Baron & Kenny, 1986); some variables may serve as both. For example, coping strategies serve as a mediator when it links stressors to the stress reaction, and as a moderator when it affects the degree of relationship between stressors and stress (Frese, 1986).

The main point of the framework is to show the key variables that should be attended to when carrying out studies of psychological acculturation. It is contended that any study that ignores any of these broad classes of variables will be incomplete, and be unable to comprehend individuals who are experiencing acculturation. For example, research that does not attend to the cultural and psychological characteristics that individuals bring to the process, merely characterizing them by name (e.g., as "Vietnamese", or "Somali", or even less helpfully as "minorities" or "immigrants"), cannot hope to understand their acculturation or adaptation. Similarly, research that ignores key features of the dominant society (such as their demography, immigration policies, and attitudes towards immigrants) is also incomplete. However, it is important to note that there is no single study that has incorporated or verified all aspects of the framework in Figure 5; it is a composite framework, assembling concepts and findings from numerous smaller scale studies.

To expand on Figure 5, we consider in detail the various situational and personal factors that are now widely believed to influence psychological acculturation.

Society of Origin. A complete study of acculturation would need to start with a fairly comprehensive examination of the two societal contexts: that of origin and that of settlement. In the society of origin, the cultural characteristics that accompany individuals into the acculturation process need description, in part to understand (literally) where the person is coming from, and in part to establish cultural features for comparison with the society of settlement as a basis for estimating an important factor to be discussed later, that of *cultural distance.* The combination of political, economic and demographic conditions being faced by individuals in their society of origin also need to be studied as a basis for understanding the degree of *voluntariness* in the *migration motivation* of acculturating individuals. Recent arguments by Richmond (1993) suggest that migrants can be ranged on a continuum between *reactive* and *proactive*, with the former being motivated by factors that are constraining or exclusionary, and generally negative in character, while the latter are motivated by factors that are facilitating or enabling, and generally positive in character; these contrasting factors have also been referred to as *push/pull* factors in the earlier literature on migration motivation.

Society of Settlement. In the society of settlement, a number of factors have importance. First there are the general orientations a society and its citizens have towards immigration and pluralism. Some have been built by immigration over the centuries, and this process may be a continuing one, guided by a deliberate immigration policy (Sabatier & Berry, 1994). The important issue to understand for the process of acculturation is both the historical and attitudinal situation faced by migrants in the society of settlement. Some societies are accepting of cultural pluralism resulting from immigration, taking steps to support the continuation of cultural diversity as a shared communal resource; this position represents a positive *multicultural ideology* (Berry & Kalin, 1995) and corresponds to the integration strategy in Figure 3. Others seek to eliminate diversity through policies and programmes of assimilation; while others attempt to segregate or marginalize diverse populations in their societies. Murphy (1965) has argued that societies supportive of cultural pluralism (that is, with a positive multicultural ideology) provide a more positive settlement context for two reasons: they are less likely to enforce cultural change (assimilation) or exclusion (segregation and marginalization) on immigrants; and they are more likely to provide social support both from the institutions of the larger society (e.g., culturally sensitive health care, and multicultural curricula in schools), and from the continuing and evolving ethnocultural communities that usually make up pluralistic societies. However, even where pluralism is accepted, there are well-known variations in the relative acceptance of specific cultural, racial and religious groups (e.g., Berry & Kalin, 1995; Hagendoorn, 1993). Those groups that are less well accepted experience hostility, rejection and discrimination, one factor that is predictive of poor long-term adaptation (Beiser et al 1988; Fernando, 1993).

Group-Level Acculturation. With respect to group acculturation, migrant groups usually change substantially as a result of living with these two sets of cultural influences. Physical changes are often profound, frequently involving urbanization, and increased population density. Biological changes include new dietary intake and exposure to new diseases, both of which have implications for the health status of the whole group. Economic changes can involve a general loss of status or new employment opportunities for the group. Social changes range from disrupted communities to new and important friendships. Finally, cultural changes (which are at the core of the notion of acculturation) range from relatively superficial changes in what is eaten or worn, to deeper ones involving language shifts, religious conversions, and fundamental alterations to value systems.

Psychological Acculturation Phenomena. The central line in Figure 5 represents the five main phenomena included in the process of *psychological acculturation* beginning with group acculturation and individual *acculturation experience* and ending with some long-term *adaptation.* This process is highly variable for two main reasons. First is the operation of moderating factors (shown in Figure 8 above and below the central line, and with dotted lines indicating moderating effects). For policy reasons it is useful to distinguish between those moderating factors that existed prior to major acculturation taking place (and hence which cannot be much changed by public policies in the society of settlement), and those that may arise during the process of acculturation (and which are controllable, to some extent). These moderating factors attach both to groups and to individuals, and can be seen as both risk factors and protective factors, depending on their degree or level. Because they influence the course of events along the central line in Figure 5 they will be discussed following presentation of this course. Second, variability in psychological acculturation exists because of the three differing views about the degree of .difficulty that is thought to exist during acculturation, that were outlined earlier ("behavioural shifts", "acculturative stress" and "psychopathology").

The five main features of psychological acculturation have received many different names in both the general and acculturation literatures. However, there is broad agreement (see e.g., Aldwin, 1994; Lazarus, 1990, 1993) that the process of dealing with life events begins with some causal agent that places a load or demand on the organism. In the acculturation literature, these demands stem from the *experience* of having to deal with two cultures in contact, and having to participate to various extents in both of them; these intercultural contact experiences are the common starting point for all of the three conceptual approaches. In some cases these experiences represent challenges that can enhance ones life opportunities. In other cases they may seriously undermine ones life chances.

Second, individuals consider the *meaning* of these experiences, evaluating and appraising them as a source of difficulty (i.e. as stressors), or as benign, sometimes even as opportunities. The outcome of this appraisal is variable across the three approaches : when acculturation experiences are judged to pose no problem for the individual, changes are likely to be rather easy and behavioural shifts will follow smoothly. This process encompasses three sub-processes : culture shedding; culture learning; and *culture conflict* (Berry, 1992). The first two involve the accidental or deliberate loss of behaviours, and their replacement by behaviours that allow the individual a better "fit" with the society of settlement. Most often thig- process has been termed *adjustment* (Ward & Kennedy, 1993a), since the adaptive changes all take place in the acculturating individual, with few changes occurring among members of the larger society. These adjustments are typically made with minimal difficulty, in keeping with the appraisal of the acculturation experiences as non-problematic. However, some degree of conflict may occur, which is usually resolved by the acculturating person yielding to the behavioural norms of the dominant groups; in this case assimilation is the most likely outcome.

When greater levels of conflict are experienced, and the experiences are judged to be problematic, but controllable and surmountable, then the *acculturative* stress paradigm is the appropriate conceptualization. In this case, individuals understand that they are facing problems resulting from intercultural contact that cannot be dealt with easily or quickly by simply adjusting or assimilating to them. Drawing on the broader stress and adaptation paradigms (e.g. Lazarus & Folkman, 1984), this approach advocates the study of the process of how individuals deal with acculturative problems on first encountering them, and over time. In this sense, acculturative stress is a stress reaction in response to life events that are, rooted in the experience of acculturation.

When acculturation experiences overwhelm the individual, creating problems that cannot be controlled or surmounted, then the *psychopathology* paradigm is the appropriate one. In this case, there is little success in dealing with acculturation, sometimes resulting in withdrawal (separation), but sometimes involving culture shedding without culture learning (resulting in marginalization).

Third, as we have noted, individuals engage in strategies that attempt to deal with the experiences that are appraised as problematic. These basic coping strategies can be understood in relation to the four acculturation strategies outlined earlier. Within the general stress and adaptation approach, other strategies have been proposed, and are linked to the notion of *coping*. Lazarus and Folkman (1984) have identified two major functions: problem-focused coping (attempting to change or solve the problem); and emotion-focused coping (attempting to regulate the emotions associated with the problem) More recently, Endler and Parker (1990) have identified a third: avoidance-oriented coping.

These analyses of coping may or may not be valid cross-culturally; Aldwin (1994) and Lazarus (1991) suggest that cross-cultural variations are likely to be present in these distinctions, and in which ones are preferred. One key distinction, made by Diaz-Guerrero

(1979), is between *active* and *passive* coping. The former seeks to alter the situation, and hence may be similar to problem-focused coping. It may have only limited success if the problem lies in the dominant society, especially if there is little interest in the dominant group in accommodating the needs of acculturating individuals. Passive coping reflects patience and self-modification, and resembles the assimilation acculturation strategy. These strategies are likely to be successful only if the dominant society has positive attitudes towards, and is willing to accept members of the acculturating groups. If attitudes are hostile, the passive coping strategy may well lead to unacceptable levels of exclusion or domination.

The fourth aspect of psychological acculturation is a complex set of immediate effects, including physiological and emotional reactions, coming closest to the notion of *stress*, as a "reaction to conditions of living" (Lazarus, 1990. p. 2). In terms of the three conceptual approaches, (shifts, stress, psychopathology), when behavioural shifts have taken place, without difficulty, stress is likely to be minimal and personal consequences are generally positive. When acculturative problems (stressors) do arise, but have been successfully coped with, stress will be similarly low and the immediate effects positive; but when stressors are not completely surmounted, stress will be higher and effects more negative. And when acculturative problems have been overwhelming, and have not been successfully dealt with, immediate effects will be substantially negative and stress levels debilitating, including personal crises, and commonly anxiety and depression.

The last of the five main features of psychological acculturation is the long-term *adaptation* that may be achieved. As we saw earlier, adaptation refers to the relatively stable changes that take place in an individual or group in response to environmental demands. Moreover, adaptation may or may not improve the "fit" between individuals and their environments. It is thus not a term that necessarily implies that individuals or groups change to become more like their environments (i.e. adjustment), but may involve resistance and attempts to change their environments or away from them altogether. In this usage, adaptation is an outcome that may or may not be positive in valence (i.e. meaning only *well-adapted*). This bi-polar sense of the concept of adaptation is used in this framework; long term adaptation to acculturation is highly variable ranging from well- to poorly- adapted, varying from a situation where individuals can manage their new lives very well, to one where they are unable to carry on in the new society.

Adaptation is also multifaceted (Aycan & Berry, 1995). The initial distinction between *psychological* and *sociocultural* adaptation has been proposed and validated by Ward and colleagues (Searle & Ward, 1990; Ward, 1996; Ward & Kennedy, 1993a). As noted previously psychological adaptation largely involves one's psychological and physical well-being (Schmitz, 1992a), while socio-cultural adaptation refers to how well an acculturating individual is able to manage daily life in the new cultural context. While conceptually distinct, they are empirically related to some extent (correlations between the two measures are in the +.4 to +.5 range). However, they are also empirically distinct in the sense that they usually have different time courses and different experiential predictors. Psychological problems often increase soon after contact, followed by a general (but variable) decrease over time; sociocultural adaptation, however, has a linear improvement with time. Analyses of the factors affecting adaptation (to be discussed below) reveal a generally consistent pattern: good psychological adaptation is predicted by personality variables, life change events and social support, while good sociocultural adaptation is predicted by cultural knowledge, degree of contact, and intergroup attitudes; both aspects of adaptation are usually predicted by the successful pursuit of the integration acculturation strategy, and by minimal cultural distance (Ward & Kennedy, 1993b; Ward, 1996). With respect to *economic adaptation* Aycan & Berry (1994) showed that psychological and socio-cultural adaptation were predicted by much the same set of variables as in Ward's studies, while economic adaptation was predicted by migration motivation, perception of relative deprivation and status loss on first entry into the work world. Further studies are needed to elaborate this economic aspect of adaptation, and how it relates to the other two (see also Hauff & Vaglum, 1993).

We are now in a position to consider the *moderating* factors that exist prior to and those that arise *during* the process of acculturation.

As noted earlier, while termed "moderating" they sometimes serve as "mediating" variables (i.e. intervene directly between the main events). Different empirical studies assign different roles to these factors; it is not possible at this point in acculturation research to unambiguously claim them to be one or the other.

Factors Existing Prior to Acculturation. Individuals begin the acculturation process with a number of personal characteristics of both a demographic and social nature. In particular one's age has a known relationship to the way acculturation will proceed. When acculturation starts early (e.g. prior to entry into primary school), the process is generally smoothe (Beiser et al, 1988). The reasons for this are not clear; perhaps full enculturation into one's parents' culture is not sufficiently advanced to require much culture shedding or to create any serious culture conflict; or perhaps personal flexibility and adaptability are maximal during these early years. However, youth do often experience substantial problems (Aronowitz, 1992; Carlin, 1990; Ghuman, 1991; Sam & Berry, 1995) particularly during adolescence. It is possible that conflicts between demands of parents and peers are maximal at this period, or that the problems of life transitions between childhood and adulthood are compounded by cultural transitions. For example, developmental issues of identity come to the fore at this time (Phinney, 1990) and interact with questions of ethnic identity, multiplying the questions about who one really is.

If acculturation begins in later life (e.g. on retirement, or when older parents migrate to join their adult offspring under family reunification programmes) there appears to be increased risk (Beiser et al 1988; Ebrahim, 1992). Perhaps the same factors of length of enculturation and adaptability suggested for children are also at work here: a whole life in one cultural setting cannot easily be ignored when attempting to live in a new one.

Gender has variable influence on the acculturation process. There is substantial evidence that females may be more at risk for problems than males (e.g. Beiser et al, 1988; Carballo, 1994). However, this generalization probably itself depends on the relative status and differential treatment of females in the two cultures: where there is a substantial difference, attempts by females to take on new roles available in the society of settlement may bring them. into conflict with their heritage culture (e.g., Moghaddam, Ditto & Taylor, 1990; Naidoo 1992; Naidoo & Davis, 1988), placing them at risk.

Education appears as a consistent factor associated with positive adaptations: higher education is predictive of lower stress (Beiser et al, 1988; Jayasuriya et al, 1992). A number of reasons have been suggested for this relationship. First, education is a personal resource in itself: problem analysis and problem solving are usually instilled by formal education and likely contribute to better adaptation. Second, education is a correlate of other resources, such as income, occupational status, support networks etc, all of which are themselves protective factors (see below). Third, for many migrants, education may attune them to features of the society into which they settle; it is a kind of pre-acculturation to the language, history, values and norms of the new culture.

Related to education is one's place in the economic world. Although high status (like education) is a resource, a common experience for migrants is a combination of status loss and limited status mobility (Aycan & Berry, 1994). One's "departure status" is frequently higher than one's "entry status"; credentials (educational and work experience) are frequently devalued on arrival (Cumming et al 1989). Sometimes this is due to real differences in qualifications, but it may also be due to ignorance and/or prejudice in the society of settlement, leading to status loss, and the risk of stress. For similar reasons, the usual main goal of migration (upward status mobility) is thwarted, leading again to risk for various disorders, such as depression (Beiser, Johnson & Turner, 1993). In a sense, these problems lie in personal qualities brought to the acculturation process, but they also reside in the interaction between the migrant and the institutions of the society of settlement; hence, problems of status loss and limited mobility can be usually addressed during the course of acculturation.

Reasons for migrating have long been studied using the concepts of *push/pull motivations* and *expectations*. As we noted earlier, Richmond (1993) has proposed that a reactive-proactive continuum of migration motivation be employed, in which push motives (including involuntary or forced migration, and negative expectations) characterize the reactive end of the dimension, while pull motives, (including voluntary migration and positive expectations) cluster at the proactive end. Such a single dimension allows for more concise conceptualization and ease of empirical analysis. Viewing previous research in this light permits some generalizations about the relationship between motives and stress and adaptation. For example, Kim (1988) found that, as usual, those with high "push" motivation had more psychological adaptation problems. However, those with high "pull" motivation had almost as great a number of problems. It appears that those who are reactive are more at risk, but so too are those who are highly proactive; it is likely they these latter migrants had extremely intense or excessively high (even unrealistic) expectations about their life in the new society, which were not met, leading to greater stress.

Cultural distance (how dissimilar the two cultures are in language, religion etc), too, lies not uniquely in the background of the acculturating individual but in the dissimilarity between the two cultures in contact. The general and consistent finding is that the greater the cultural differences, the less positive is the adaptation. This is the case for sojourners and immigrants (Ward & Searle, 1991; Ward & Kennedy, 1992) and for indigenous people (Berry, 1976). Greater cultural distance implies the need for greater culture shedding and culture learning, and perhaps large differences trigger negative intergroup attitudes, and induce greater culture conflict leading to poorer adaptation.

Personal factors have also been shown to affect the course of acculturation. In the personality domain, a number of traits have been proposed as both risk and protective factors, including locus of control and, introversion/extraversion (Ward & Kennedy, 1992), and self-efficacy (Schwarzer et al, 1994). However, consistent findings have been rare, possibly because, once again, it is not so much the trait by itself but its "fit" with the new cultural setting that matters. Kealey (1989) has advocated such a person x situation approach to studying sojourner adaptation.

One finding (Schmitz, 1994), among a group of immigrants to Germany, is that stress reaction styles are related to a person's preferred acculturation strategy. Using the Grossarth-Maticek and

Eysenck (1990) Psycho-Social Stress Inventory, the "Approach" style was positively related to a preference for Assimilation, "Avoidance" to Separation, "Flexible" to Integration, and "Psychopathology" to Marginalization.

Factors Arising During Acculturation. It is now clear that the phase of acculturation needs to be taken into account if stress and adaptation are to be understood. That is, how long a person has been experiencing acculturation strongly affects the kind and extent of problems. The classical description of positive adaptation in relation to time has been in terms of a U-curve. Only a few problem are present early, followed by more serious problems later, and finally a more positive long-term adaptation is achieved. However, there is little empirical evidence for such a standard course, nor for fixed times (in terms of months or years) when such variations will occur. Church (1982; p. 542) has concluded that support for the U-curve is "weak, inconclusive and overgeneralized", although there are occasional longitudinal studies suggesting fluctuations in stress over time (e.g., Klineberg, 1980; Zheng & Berry, 1991; Hurh & Kim, 1990; Ward & Kennedy, 1995; Beiser, 1994).

An alternative to a fixed, stage-like conceptualization of the relationship between length of acculturation and problems experienced is to consider the specific nature of the experiences and problems encountered as they change over time (e.g. initially learning a language, obtaining employment and housing, followed by establishing social relationships and recreational opportunities) and the relationship of such problems to the personal resources of the migrant and to opportunities in the society of settlement (Ho, 1995). This approach emphasizes the high degree of variability to be expected over the time course from initial contact to eventual long-term adaptation.

Acculturation strategies have been shown to have substantial relationships with positive adaptation: integration is usually the most successful; marginalization is the least; and assimilation and separation strategies are intermediate. This pattern has been found in virtually every study, and is present for all types of acculturating groups (Berry, 1990a; Berry & Sam, 1997. Why this should be so, however, is not clear. In one interpretation, the integration strategy incorporates many of the other protective factors: a willingness for mutual accommodation (i.e. the presence of mutual positive attitudes), and absence of prejudice and discrimination - see below); involvement in two cultural communities (i.e. having two social support systems - see below); and being flexible in personality. In sharp contrast, marginalization involves rejection by the dominant society, combined with own-culture loss; this means the presence of hostility and much reduced social support. Assimilation involves own-culture shedding (even though it may be voluntary), and separation involves rejection of the dominant culture (perhaps reciprocated by them). In the simplest version of this explanation, integration involves two positive orientations, marginalization involves two negative ones, while assimilation and separation involve one positive and one negative relationship.

Another possible reason for the finding that Integration is the most adaptive strategy is that most studies of the relationship between acculturation strategies and adaptation have been carried out in multicultural societies. That is, there could be benefits to persons matching their acculturation strategies to that generally advocated and accepted in the larger society. However, in recent studies in societies that are more "Melting Pot" or assimilationist in orientation, the Integration strategy remained the most adaptive (and conversely marginalization was the least adaptive) strategy. For example this was the case among Indian immigrants to.the USA (Krishnan & Berry, 1992), and Third World immigrant youth in Norway (Sam & Berry, 1995); and Schmitz (1992b, p.368), working with a variety of immigrant groups in Germany, concluded that "The findings suggest that integration seems to be the most effective strategy if we take long term health and well-being as indicators".

Related to acculturation strategies are the coping strategies discussed earlier. Some empirical evidence supports the relationship between coping and acculturation strategies. For example, in the same study Schmitz (1992) found, using the three coping styles identified by Endler and Parker (1990) that integration is positively correlated with task orientation, segregation is positively correlated with emotion and avoidance orientation, and assimilation is positively correlated with both task and emotion orientation, but negatively with avoidance orientation. And, as we have just noted these strategies were.related to health outcomes for immigrants to Germany.

In the field of psychological well-being generally, the variable of social support has been widely studied (Lin, Dean & Ensel, 1986). Its role in adaptation to acculturation has also been supported (e.g. Furnham & Alibhai, 1985; Furnham & Shiekh, 1993; Jayasuriya, Sang & Fielding, 1992; Vega & Rumbaut, 1991). For some, links to one's heritage culture (i.e. with co-nationals) are associated with lower stress (e.g., Vega et al, 1991; Ward & Kennedy, 1993b), for others links to members of the society of settlement are more helpful, particularly if relationships match one's expectations (e.g., Berry & Kostovcik, 1990); but in most studies, supportive relationships with both cultures are most predictive of successful adaptation (Berry et al 1987; Kealey, 1989). This latter finding corresponds to observations made earlier about the advantages of the integration strategy.

It has been widely reported that the experience of prejudice and discrimination has a significant negative effect on a person's well-being (e.g., Fenton, 1989; Halpern, 1993). In groups experiencing acculturation this can be an added risk factor (Beiser et al, 1988). Murphy (1965) has argued that such prejudice is likely to be less prevalent in culturally plural societies, but it is by no means absent (e.g., Berry & Kalin, 1995). Indeed Fernando (1993) has designated racism as the most serious problem and risk factor facing immigrants and their mental health.

Overview of the Empirical Evidence

The first two sections of this paper established the two broad socio-political contexts (multiculturalism and immigration), while the last two sections outlined the main issues with respect to intergroup relations and acculturation. In this section we present an overview of what,is known, from empirical studies in social and cultural psychology about the current situation in Canada. We begin by examining evidence about ethnic and race relations. We then turn to evidence about patterns of psychological acculturation and how these may affect the larger society.

Ethnic and Race Relations

This section contains three major chunks of information. First are some *general indicators of acceptance of cultural diversity:* do Canadian like living in a heterogeneous society, do they enjoy intercultural differences and encounters? Second are some *specific intergroup attitudes*, based on a single measure of how comfortable people are being around those of various specific ethnic backgrounds. And finally, how people *identity themselves* (in civic or ethnic terms), and how much they identify with the nation state of Canada are examined. In most cases, the information will be presented aggregated by ethnic origin of respondent (British, French, or other) and region of residence (inside or outside Quebec).

General Orientations. Two scales are of interest: *Multicultural Ideology* and *Tolerance-Prejudice.* In the national population as a whole, both the acceptance of multiculturalism, and level of tolerance (essentially the opposite to prejudice) are moderately high, and the long term trends have been for both to increase over the pact 15 years. On the 7-point response scale used, the means were 4.59 and 5.37 respectively. When analysed by ethnic origin and region, Figures 6 and 7 show the resulting pattern (Berry & Kahn, 1995).

While there are some similarities in the distribution of these two general orientations (e.g., no effect of ethnic origin), there are some important differences. Most evident is the presence of a regional effect for Tolerance-Prejudice, but an interaction effect for Multicultural Ideology; this difference indicates that dissimilar explanations are needed to account for the two scores. For Tolerance-Prejudice, it may be that where intergroup relations are contentious (e.g. in Quebec) all groups are relatively less tolerant. For Multicultural Ideology, a kind of self-interest, seems to account for the distribution: where people are advantaged by policies and programmes supporting multiculturalism (e.g., British and Others inside Quebec; French outside Quebec) support is high; but where people may be threatened by pluralist policies (e.g., French in Quebec) support for diversity is lower.

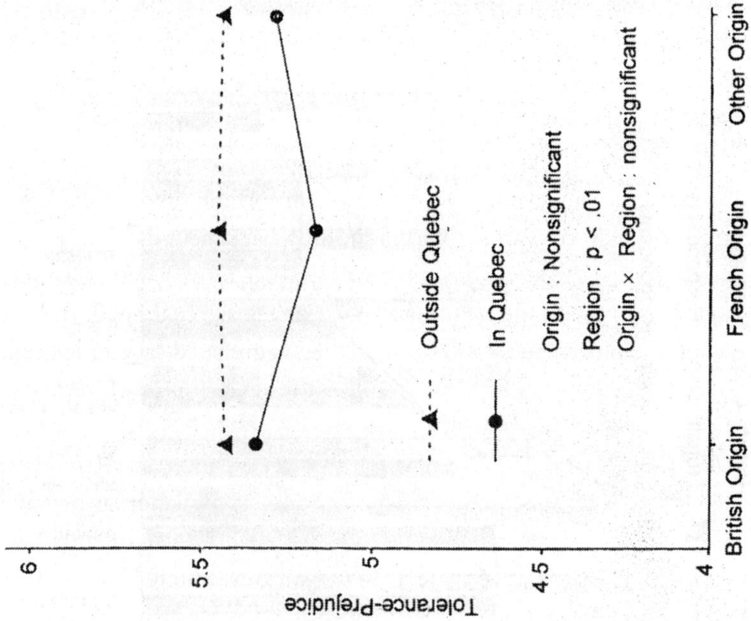
Tolerance-Prejudice
6
5.5
5
4.5
4
British Origin
French Origin
Other Origin
Outside Quebec
In Quebec
Origin : Nonsignificant
Region : p < .01
Origin × Region : nonsignificant

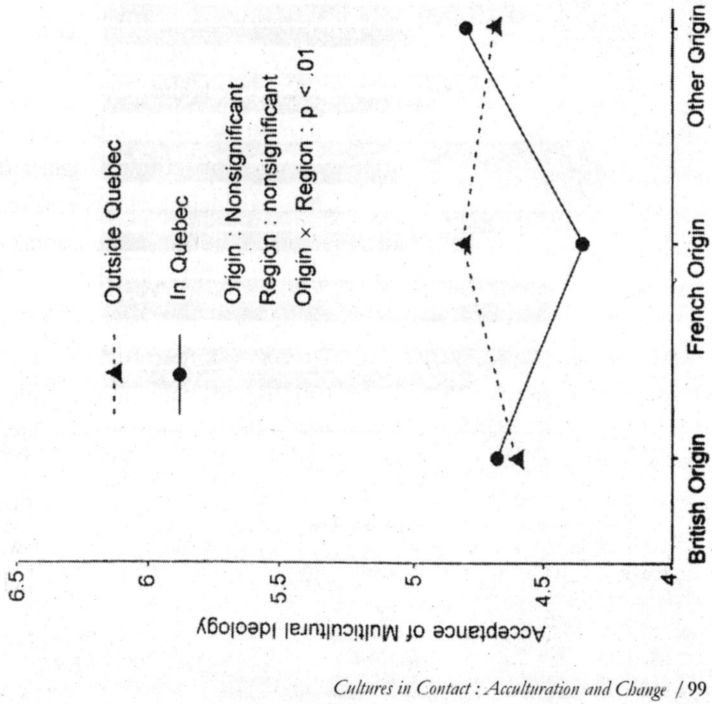
Acceptance of Multicultural Ideology
6.5
6
5.5
5
4.5
4
British Origin
French Origin
Other Origin
Outside Quebec
In Quebec
Origin : Nonsignificant
Region : nonsignificant
Origin × Region : p < .01

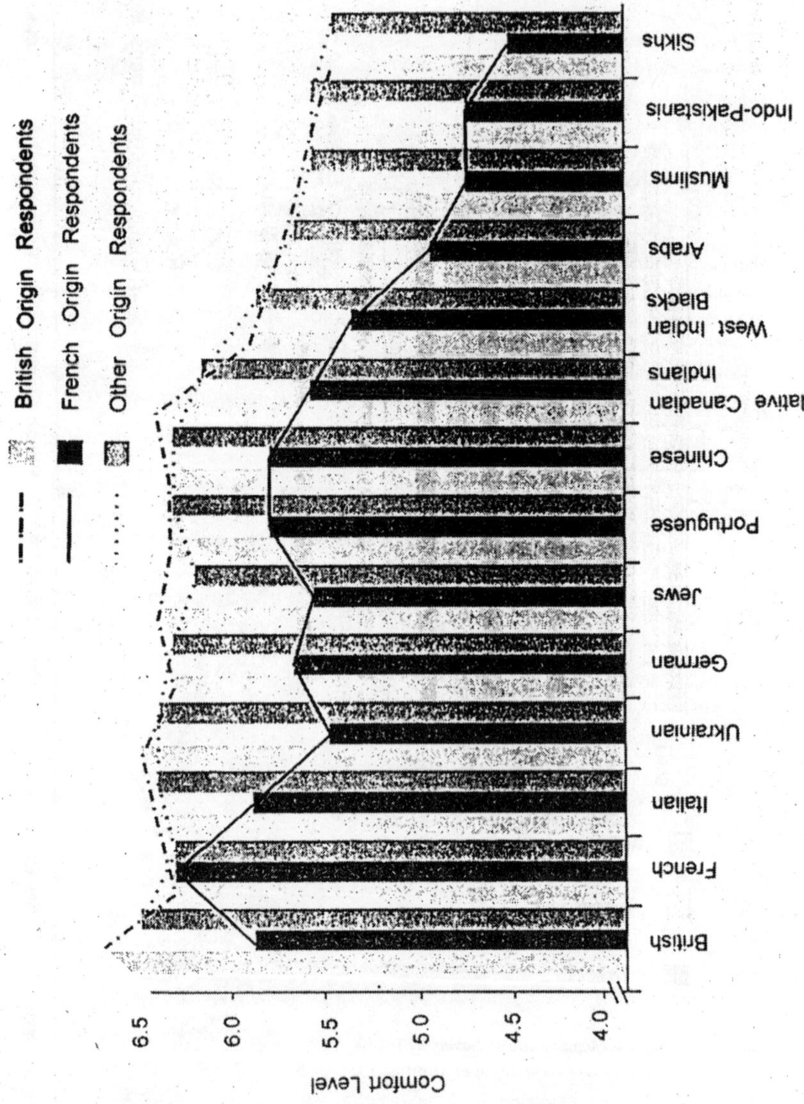

Fig. 8 : Mean Comfort Levels by Ethnic Origin of Respondents in the National Sample

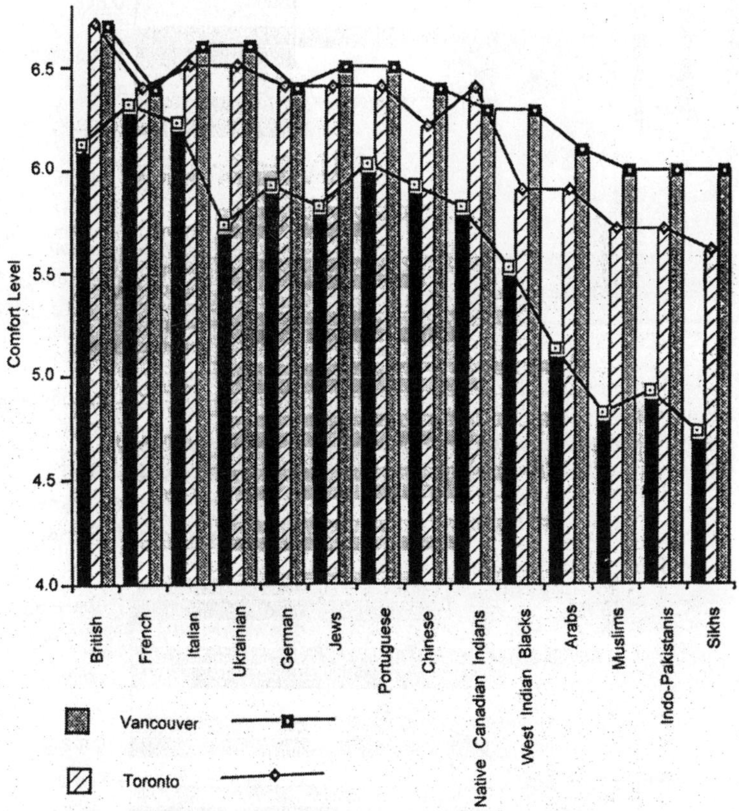

Fig. 9 : Mean Comfort Levels by Ethnic Origin of Respondents in the National Sample in Montreal, Toronto and Vancouver

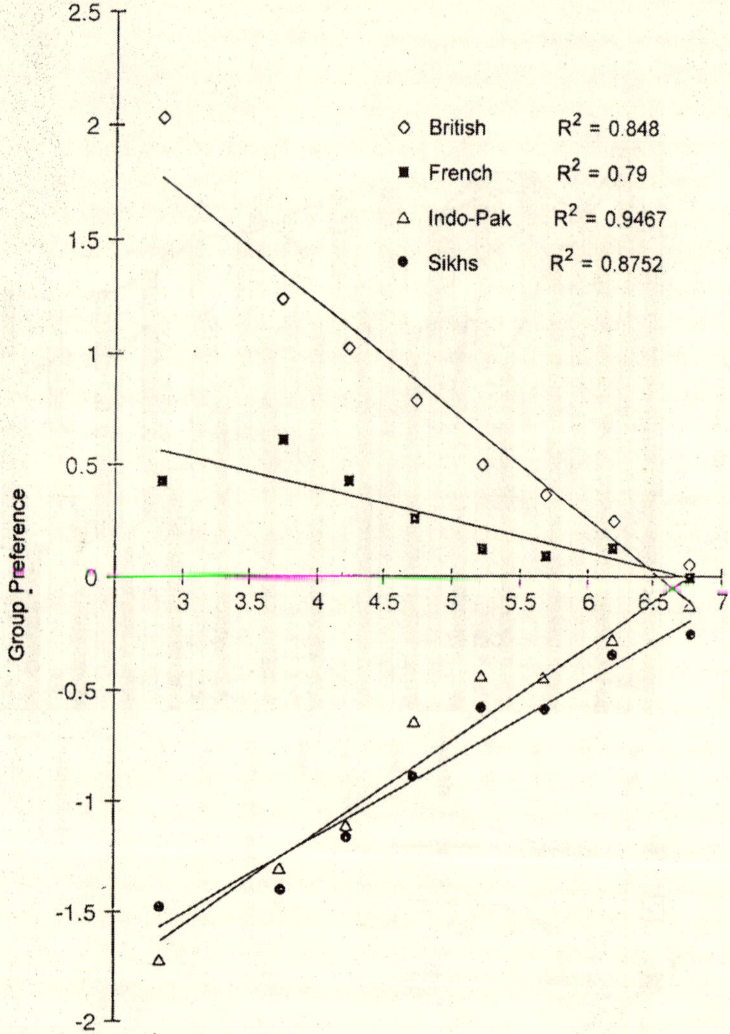

Fig. 10 : Positive or Negative Group Preference in British Origin Sample, as a Function of Tolerance

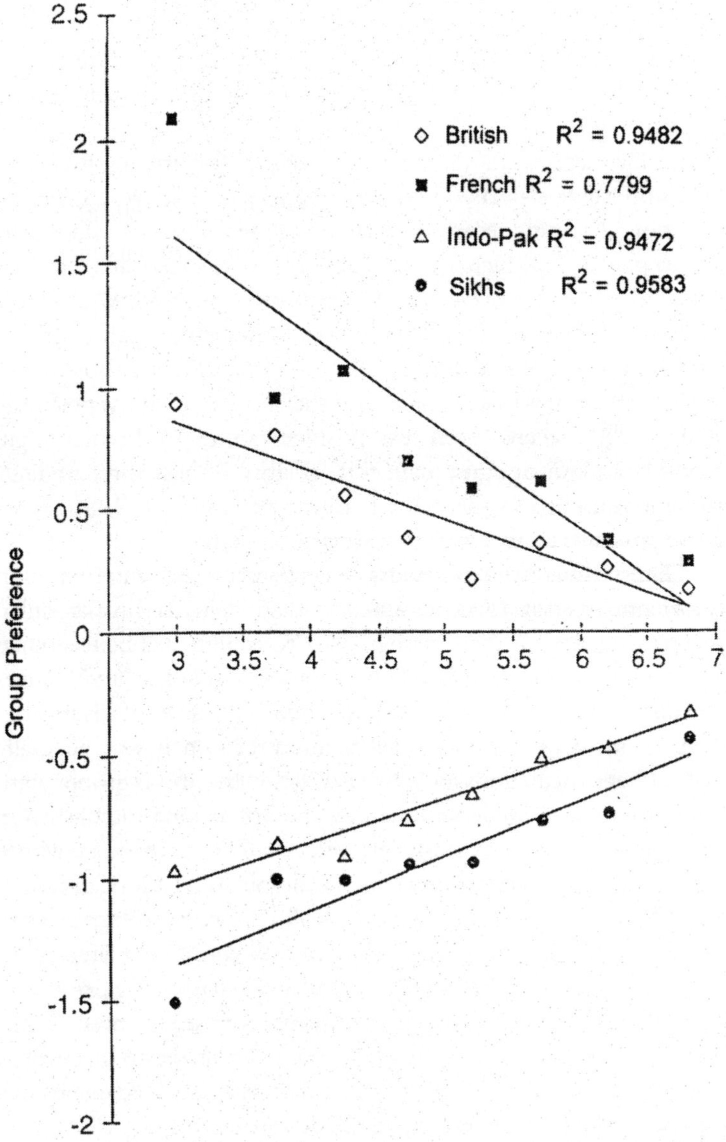

Fig. 11 : Positive or Negative Group Preference in French Origin Sample, as a Function of Tolerance

Ethnic Attitudes. Respondents indicated their degree of comfort being around persons of selected ethnic background. Figures 8 and 9 show these "comfort levels" according to ethnic origin of the respondent (in the total sample), and for three major urban centres (N = 500 each) not broken down by ethnicity (Berry & Kalin, 1995).

In the data from the national sample (Figure 8), there are three important aspects. First, while comfort levels were generally high, not all groups received the same ratings. There is a hierarchy of acceptance in which British- through to Native-Canadians are evaluated more positively than other groups. Second, while there are no differences between British- and Other- origin ratings, those given by French-origin respondents are noticeably less positive. A third observation is that those groups that are generally less positively rated tend to receive even less positive ratings by French-origin respondents. For the three main cities (Figure 9) these three findings are repeated, but possibly with a steeper drop-off in Montreal for those groups that are lower in general acceptance.

There is thus a clear hierarchy of acceptance, but its interpretation is not entirely clear. One possibility is that Prejudice (in particular, racism) accounts for these ratings. This possibility will be examined below, but it can be noted here that Chinese-Canadians and Native-Canadians are as generally highly rated as those of European background; thus, a simple racism interpretation is not generally valid. Other explanations include: *familiarity* with various groups, with those groups who are less numerous and not as long-established in Canada being rated less positively; and *similarity*, with those whose cultural origins are less similar to the dominant (European-based) population being rated less positively. These two basic explanatory concepts in social psychology will be further considered later.

Since there may have been extraneous factors (e.g., response style) affecting the use of the comfort level scale, these scores were standardized (with zero being the average rating given by a respondent to all 14 groups; attitudes are then expressed as positive or negative deviation from this mean of zero).

These standardized ethnic attitude scores can be related to scores on the Tolerance-Prejudice scale. Figures 10 and 11 show these relationships for British- and French-origin Canadians separately, using attitudes toward British-, French-, Ind°Pakistani- and Sikh-Canadians. Note that while the most Tolerant respondents make very little distinction between any groups, the least Tolerant individuals make the greatest distinction between their attitudes towards the two "charter" groups and the two South Asian groups. Importantly, evenly the least Tolerant British and French origin respondents maintain a positive attitude toward the other "charter" group; that is, they seem to serve as *positive reference groups* for each other.

Ethnic and Civic Identities. The third area of interest is how people identify themselves. The 1991 survey had three questions: an ethnic *origin* question (similar to the 1991 Census question); an *identity* question (how they usually thought of themselves), with various ethnic options provided, based on answers to the first question, along with regional and national options (e.g., "Quebecois", "Canadian"); and a *strength* of identification (on a 7-point scale) analysed for three identities ("Canadian"! "Canadien"; provincial; ethnic). Related to these identity questions, was a scale of *Canadianism* attempting to assess ones sense of attachment and commitment to Canada.

Responses to the identity questions are presented in Table 1 according to respondents ethnic origin for both the 1974 and 1991 surveys, and in Table 2 for strength of identification by region, for 1991 only (Kalin and Berry, 1995).

Table 1

Self-Identity (in percents) of Respondents in Two National Surveys by Ethnic Origin

Self-Identity	MAS 74				MAS 91			
	Ethnic Origin				Ethnic Origin			
	Tot.	Bri.	Fr.	OEth	Tot.	Bri.	Fr.	OEth
Canadian/Canadien	59	80	26	59	64	80	32	65
British-Canadian	7	13	3	3	2	6	0	0
French-Canadian	15	3	47	3	4	1	16	0
Provincial [b]	7	1	22	1	19	9	47	9
Other-Ethnic-Can.	8	0	0	28	7	1	1	20
Other National	3	2	2	5	4	3	4	5
N =	1810	708	376	541	3276	1392	746	1027

Table 2
Mean Strength of Identification with Three Identities
by Region of Resisdence in 1991 Survey[a]

Identity	Regions					
	TOT.	ATL	QUE	ONT	PRAI	BCh
Canadian/Canadien[b]	6.3	6.7	5.2[d]	6.6	6.6	6.7
Provincial	5.3	5.8	6.0	4.4[e]	5.5	5.5
"Ethnic" Origin[c]	4.1	3.5	4.6[f]	3.9	4.1	4.0
N =	3320	300	863	1191	584	382

In both the 1974 and 1991 surveys (Table 1) the most frequent identity was "Canadian"/"Canadien"; however, this was more the case among British- and Other-origin, than among French-origin, respondents. Among the latter, the most frequent identity in 1974 was "Canadien-Frangais", but this mostly shifted to a provincial (largely "Quebecois") identity in 1991, and somewhat less to a "Canadien" identity. "Other Ethnic" identities were the third most frequent, but declined from 1974 to 1991.

While some (e.g., Balthazar, 1995) claim that a Quebecois identity is in essence a pluralistic "civic" or "territorial" identity, and not limited to a single (i.e. French) ethnic origin, it is not clear that this transition from an ethnic to a civic identity has yet been accomplished (Breton, 1988). Indeed, evidence contrary to this claim occasionally appears in pronouncements by public figures,' and is apparent in the October 1995 Referendum polls.

There appears to be no important variation (in Table 2) in strength of identification as "Canadian"/"Canadien". However, respondents in Quebec had a lower strength rating for this identity, combined with a slightly higher strength rating for a "Provincial" (i.e. "Quebecois") identity.

When these, identities are related to the two general orientations within the three ethnic-origin categories, some variations do appear (Kalin & Berry, 1995). For British-origin respondents, those with a "Provincial" identity were lower than those with other identities on Tolerance (but not on Multicultural Ideology). The reverse was true for French-origin respondents: those with a "Provincial" identity were lower than those with other identities on Multicultural Ideology (but not on Tolerance). As one might expect, among Other-origin Canadians, those with an "Ethnic" identity were most supportive of a Multicultural Ideology, while those with a "Provincial" Identity were least Tolerant. Most importantly, there is no evidence that those who identify as "Canadian" are less supportive of diversity. Findings for the Canadianism scale are shown in Figure 12, according to ethnic origin and region of residence.

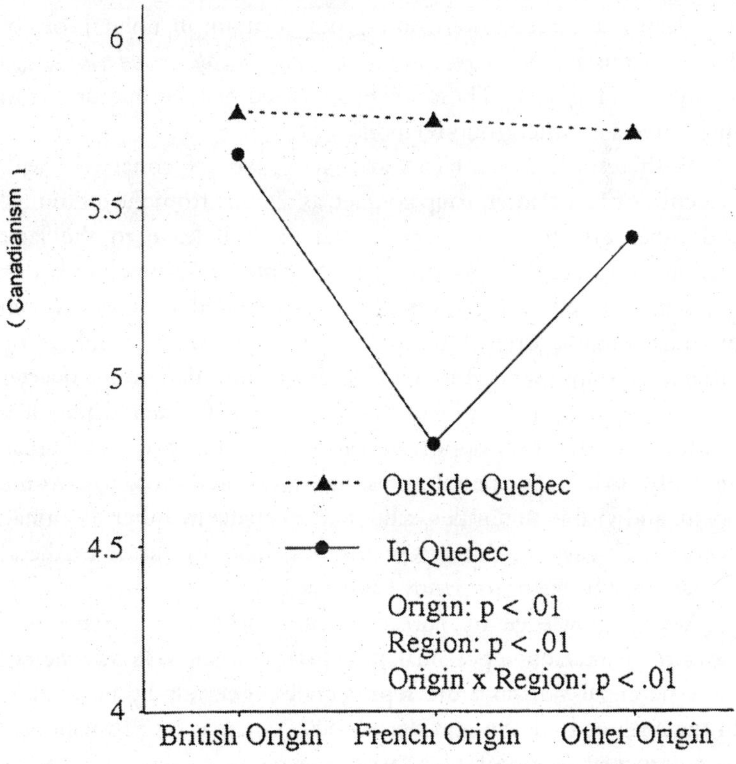

Fig. 12 : Distribution of Mean Scores on Canadianism by Ethnic Origin and Region of Residence of Respondents

Unlike the two other scale distributions, scores on Canadianism vary significantly by Ethnic Origin, and Region, and in their interaction (Figure 12). All three features are evidently due to the lower score on the scale among French-origin respondents living in Quebec. When these scale scores are related to the three identity categories, a common and significant pattern appears in all three ethnic-origin groups: those with a "Provincial" identity score low on Canadianism, and (not surprisingly) those with a "Canadian" identity score higher. And for British- and Other-origin groups, those with an "Ethnic" identity do not score lower on the Canadianism scale, indicating that the much-maligned "hyphenated identity" is no threat to one's attachment to Canada.

Earlier, we outlined some domains and issues that assume central importance in understanding intergroup relations in a plural society. Two domains are *contact and sharing*; and *group acceptance and tolerance* (as identified in Figure 1). These will be reviewed first, before turning to their effects on intergroup relations.

With respect to contact and sharing, we are concerned with evidence of actual intergroup contact, as distinct from the attitudinal and other effects of contact, which we will leave to the later section. What are the opportunities for contact? Although Canada's population is ethnically diverse, it is distributed in a way which provides variable opportunities for contact between members of different groups. While French-Canadians comprise over a quarter of the population, there are many areas of Canada where few reside; hence the sheer opportunity to have contact may be minimal. Similarly, with Native peoples who are distributed more toward the north, and visible minorities, who tend to reside in either Montreal, Toronto, Calgary or Vancouver, the possibility of direct firsthand contact may be slight for many Canadians.

While knowledge of contact opportunities is important as a measure of interaction potential, it is also important to know whether these potential situations are represented cognitively by individuals. In the analysis by Kalin and Berry (1982a), ratings by non-members of a particular group of how "well-known" the group was to them exhibited substantial group-level correlations with census-established percentages of those groups in the respondents' district. Thus, it appears that individuals are well aware of the ethnicity of those (other than their own group) who live in their immediate surroundings.. That is, ethnic percentage statistics are not simply a mere census statistic; they are perceived and subjectively represented by others.

With respect to tolerance, to what extent is there variation in acceptance of different ethnic groups in Canada? More generally, what is the degree of tolerance in Canadian society, how is it to be conceptualized and how is it distributed? The attitudinal evidence is quite clear on the first question: not all groups are accorded the same degree of acceptance (Berry, et al. 1977; see Table 1). These studies showed that the most acceptable are the two charter groups (British-, French- Canadians) followed by those of North European ancestry, then Eastern and Southern European, and finally by East Asians, South Asian, West Indian and Native Canadians. While there are exceptions to this generalization (for example Japanese-Canadians tend to receive more positive attitudes than this general characterization indicates), there is widespread evidence (Palmer, 1975) that this situation has existed historically, and is related to a group's prestige (Pineo, 1977). The most recent survey (Berry & Kalin, 1995) confirms the continuation of this hierarchy, with the exception that Native and West Indian Canadians now have more acceptance than South Asian Canadians.

To some extent this hierarchy of group acceptance is due to those most numerous in the population rendering generally more positive own-group evaluations; thus, the hierarchy parallels closely the percentage representation of each group in the Canadian population. However, analyses (Berry & Kalin, 1979; Kalin & Berry, 1996) which controls for own-group (or ethnocentric) self-evaluations, tends to show that this ethnic hierarchy is generally shared by most groups, and is independent of who is asked for their evaluations of groups other than their own.

At a more general level, beyond that of attitudes towards specific groups, there is evidence that tolerance varies by ethnic group (Berry et al., 1977; Berry & Kalin, 1995 : Gouvernement du Quebec, 1996): those of British ancestry tend to exhibit more general ethnic tolerance than those of French ancestry. However, socioeconomic Status also affects the distribution of ethnic tolerance, and may account, in part for this ethnic group difference.

Some local studies have also suggested that attitudes toward non-white groups continue to be more negative than toward whites. For example, studies by Henry and Ginsberg (1985) and

Henry (1989) in Toronto demonstrate job discrimination against Black and Indo-Pakistani Canadians. In these two studies, there were two conditions: an in-person job application, and a telephone approach. In the former condition, white Canadians (non-accented), white immigrants (accented), West Indians, and Indo-Pakistanis (both accented) made phone enquiries. In the 1985 study, there was evidence of substantial job discrimination against non-whites in both conditions. However, in the 1989 study, black in-person applicants received the same number of job offers as whites, but there was evidence that whites were treated better (more politely etc). In the telephone condition, however, the 1989 results still exhibited evidence of discrimination, with white Canadians being told that the job was still open more than white immigrants, West Indians or Indo-Pakistanis.

In another study in Toronto by Breton et al (1990), two questions were asked, one of members of various ethnic groups about how they perceived their acceptance by neighbours, and the other of members of "Majority Canadians" about accepting those of other groups as neighbours. The results indicate variation by group in how accepted the various groups see themselves: West Indian-, Chinese- and Jewish- Canadians are lower; while German-, Ukrainian- Portuguese and Italian-Canadians are higher. This pattern is generally repeated with attitudes expressed by Majority Canadians.

Work by Kalin (1981) on the effect of accent on job suitability ratings shows discrimination, but in two directions : both West Indians and South Asians were rated relatively low in suitability for a high status job (plant foreman), but relatively high in suitability for a low status job (plant cleaner).

In summary, there is clear-cut evidence that ethnic attitudes towards groups vary widely, a suggestion that general ethnic tolerance varies by ethnicity, and that discrimination (while possibly declining; see Bibby, 1987) remains a problem for some groups under some conditions.

When the multiculturalism policy states that "confidence in one's own individual identity" can provide a basis for "respect for that of others and a willingness to share ideas, attitudes and assumptions", there are two assumptions made. One is that own group development and maintenance permits a sense of confidence which will lead to other group acceptance and tolerance; this we have called the *multicultural assumption* (Berry, et al, 1977, p.192), and was shown at the top of Figure 1. The other is that group development and maintenance permits group sharing. In this section we will consider the first of these assumptions, and return later to the other.

What evidence do we have that confidence in one's identity leads to ethnic tolerance, or conversely, do we know that threats to one's identity nurture intolerance? In answering this question we need to distinguish between two forms of "confidence". If we mean simply "own group glorification" or "strongly positive ingroup attitudes", then ethnocentrism theory (LeVine & Campbell, 1972) predicts an opposite relationship to that assumed in the policy. Indeed, in the national survey conducted by Berry, et al., (1977) the more positively one rated one's own group, the more negatively one rated all other groups (except in the case of Angloceltic-Canadians and French-Canadians where a positive correlation obtained). The work of Brewer and Campbell (1976) and many others attests to the near universality of this typically negative, or ethnocentric, pattern.

However, the multiculturalism policy does not appear to intend to develop confidence by own-group glorification. If we render the notion of confidence as a "sense of security" or as "self-esteem", then there is some evidence of a positive correlation with ethnic tolerance. In the general literature (Bagley, 1979), and with children (Aboud & Skerry, 1984) there is clear evidence that those with higher self-esteem tend to be more accepting of other ethnic groups. In the Berry et al (1977) study, "confidence" was measured by two scales: one involved "cultural security" (the degree to which Angloceltic- and French-Canadians did not feel Culturally or linguistically threatened by multiculturalism); and the other involved "economic security" (the degree to which these same groups did not feel that their Jobs and wages were threatened by immigration). For both security measures, there was a pattern of consistent, positive correlations with a variety of measures of general ethnic tolerance; however, the relationships with attitudes toward specific ethnic groups, while generally positive, were not so strong. of particular interest is that both security measures correlate negatively with attitudes toward one's own group among Angloceltic and French-Canadians.

More recent work with measuring security has revealed a consistent pattern of relationships between both cultural and economic security, and tolerance. In a study of members of the Alliance for the Preservation of English in Canada (APEC), Berry and Bourcier (1989) found that perceived threat and feelings of insecurity about one's cultural place in Canadian society, and about one's economic prospects, were the most substantial predictors of negative attitudes toward official bilingualism and toward French-Canadians. Similarly, Cameron and Berry (1990) found in a sample of community college students that feelings of cultural and economic security, and of high self-esteem, were important predictors of the acceptance of immigrants and refugees in Canada. This finding has been replicated by Esses et al, (1997).

These studies, mainly among dominant populations, show that the relationship between a sense of security in one's own cultural place is consistently associated with tolerance toward those who are culturally different. Since the multiculturalism policy seeks to promote confidence in one's identity among *all* Canadians, it is important to know that this psychological phenomenon appears to exist independently of which groups (dominant or non-dominant) are examined.

Thus, there appears to be some support for the multicultural assumption when confidence in one's identity is understood as a sense of security, or as self-esteem. However, if understood as own group or self glorification, then ethnic attitudes are not more positive under these conditions. Clearly, what must be promoted by programmes implementing the policy is a non-ethnocentric pride in one's group, one that recognizes the positive qualities but also the limitations, and the group's uniqueness and distinctiveness as well as the commonalities with others. It now becomes clear why the contact and sharing component is a part of the policy as well as the own group development component; without this contact, isolation, and a lack of perspective on one's own group qualities and defects is the likely result, leading to the ethnocentric pattern.

In addition to the multicultural assumption and ethnocentric relationship between these two policy components there is in principle the possibility that if a group becomes well-developed in Canadian society it may be the target of envy. This possibility reverses the direction of relationship which is anticipated by the policy, but it should not be overlooked as a possible outcome. If a group develops to the point where some might view it as "too successful", do members of that group become the object of resentment and backlash (see second line from top in Figure 1) rather than being admired for their achievement? Historically, anti-Semitism has been explained in part in these terms. At the present time religious groups with the highest educational attainment in Canada are the Jewish and Hindu religions, while those of Asian ethnic origin are also high in educational attainment. While no current research is known regarding this issue, backlash is a possible alternative to the improvement in ethnic relations anticipated in the policy, and should not be overlooked.

The validity of the *contact hypothesis* appears to be assumed in the policy: that group contact will be positively associated with group acceptance. However, as we have noted a number of other factors govern this assumed relationship. Studies of the contact hypothesis in Canada are generally supportive. For example, in a further analysis of the 1977 data base, Kalin and Berry (1982a) examined the question of contact within census tracts (essentially neighbourhoods). As we saw earlier, this analysis showed that ethnicity is being signalled accurately, as evidenced by the strong correlations between percentage ethnic group composition and ratings (by non-members) of the target group on how well-known they were. The same kind of question is possible with evaluative ratings : are non-members more or less positive in their attitudes as a function of the percentage composition of a particular ethnic group in their neighbourhood? Early studies in the United States (of white's attitudes toward blacks) suggests that there is an "ideal ratio" required to achieve positive attitudes, but beyond this proportion there is a "tipping point" where attitudes become more negative.

The results of Kalin and Berry (see Figure 13) indicate a linear positive relationship generally for the groups in their study (German-, Italian-, Ukrainian-, and French-Canadians evaluated by non-members, French-Canadians by Anglocelts outside Quebec; French-Canadians by others outside Quebec; and English-Canadians

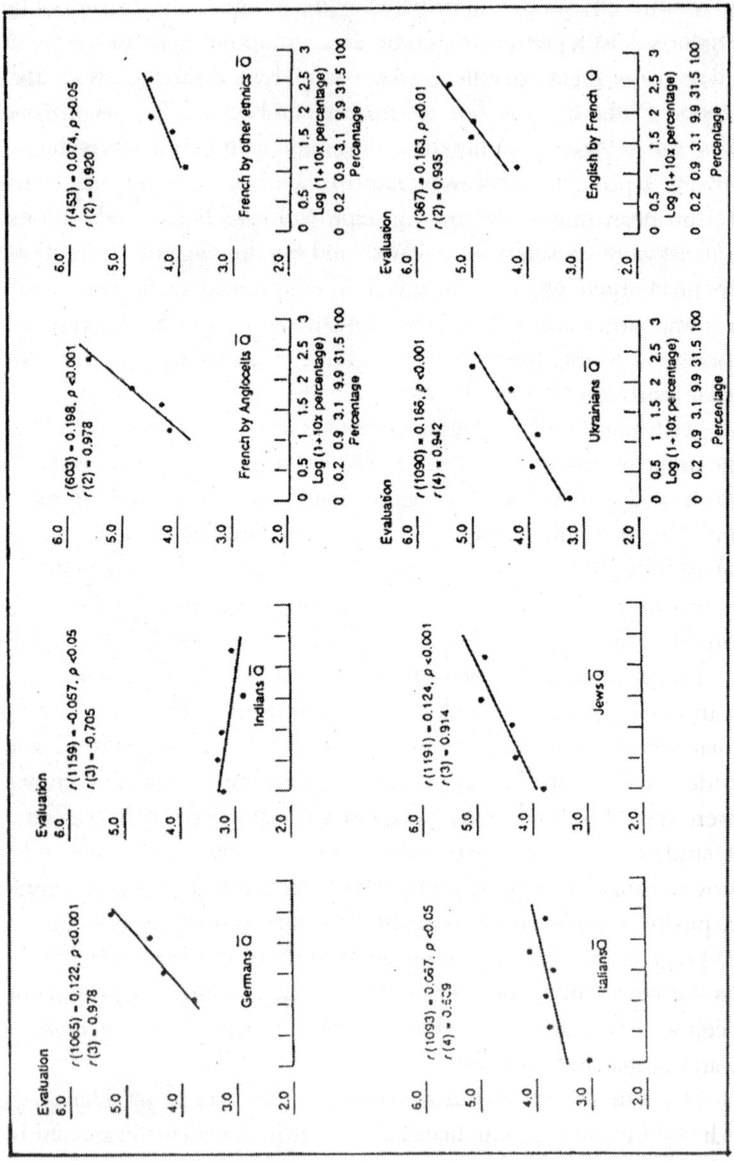

Fig. 13 : Attitudes Toward Various Ethnic Groups by Non-Members f Those Groups, as a Function of the Grroup's Percentage Presence in the Respondent's Neighbourhood (Source: Kalin & Berry, 1982)

by French-Canadians inside Quebec). The one exception is the evaluation of Canadian Indians by others; here there is a linear, but negative, relationship. We concluded that contact probably enhances positive attitudes, at least in residential neighbourhoods where contact is generally voluntary and at roughly equal status. However, in no case was percentage composition higher than 20%, and so the possibility of a "tipping point" above that figure remains a possibility. Moreover, all the groups (except one) were of European origin; and the one non-European group (Canadian Indians) were viewed more negatively as their proportion increased. It is not known whether this different relationship is due to "race" or some other factor (Such as perceived competition based on Aboriginal Rights; or on maintenance of cultural distinctiveness, either through non-participation in the larger society, or by marginalization, both of which would reduce perceived similarity; see Berry & Wells, 1992). Hence, it is not possible to generalize this single exception to other racially distinctive groups in Canada. However, a parallel analysis of the 1991 survey data by Kalin (1996) shows that the positive relationship between percentage composition and attitudes (comfort levels) is not present for other non-European cultural groups.

In the studies reviewed, some of the controlling conditions were clearly present. For example, in the social ecology study, roughly equal status (as well as voluntariness) likely characterizes most residential neighbourhoods in Canada; individuals tend to settle where they feel at home, and the census tracts selected as the units of study tend to be constructed by Statistics Canada to represent fairly homogeneous status areas. Whether contact and acceptance are positively correlated beyond these particular groups and research methods is an urgent and practical question. For, as Amir (1976) has pointed out, programmes designed to bring about mutual acceptance through mutual acquaintance can easily backfire, leading to an increase in intolerance.

Psychological Acculturation. Three major topics are addressed in this section: acculturation attitudes, behavioural shifts and acculturative stress. Not everyone in the acculturation arena has the same views about how the process should take place - or adopt the same strategies for engaging the process. *Attitudes toward* acculturation can be held by individuals in both the immigrant groups and the larger society. These have been conceptualized and assessed in Canada following the frameworks outlined earlier in Figures 3 and 4. For the larger society, Canadian official views are expressed through multiculturalism policies (both Federal and Provincial), while individual views are expressed through the *multicultural ideology* held by Canadian citizens. This latter was assessed by Berry et al (1977). While there was considerable variation across regional and ethnic groups, there was moderate acceptance of the multicultural option, combined with moderate rejection of the two alternatives of Assimilation and Separation; Views about Marginalization were not assessed in that study.

For acculturating groups in Canada (see Berry et al, [989 for a detailed review: and Lambert et.al., 1986 and Moghaddam et al. 1989 for specific studies), ethno-cultural groups generally accept multiculturalism, and individual attitudes favoured Integration, while rejecting the other three alternatives. For French-Canadians outside Quebec, Portuguese-Canadians, Korean-Canadians and Hungarian-Canadians, the rank order was generally the same: Integration was most preferred, followed either by Assimilation or Separation, and with Marginalization clearly unacceptable. A similar pattern has also been found for Aboriginal peoples in Canada (Berry, 1980b). However, for South Asian immigrant women in Montreal, Moghaddam and Taylor (1987) have reported some degree of ambivalence with respect to heritage culture maintenance in general, while at the same time showing strong support for some particular aspects of heritage culture.

We thus have a rather'clear coinciding of views at the present time in Canada. All four levels of orientations toward acculturation (i.e. in the larger society and acculturating groups, and at both the policy and individual attitudinal levels) are generally positive toward Integration, while rejecting the other alternatives to varying degrees. This broad consensus provides a baseline upon which to seek to improve intergroup relations in Canada. As we saw earlier, for intergroup contact to result in more positive mutual attitudes, there needs to be some shared superordinate goals. This consensus about how groups should relate to each other (Integration) is one such common goal: that is the view that all peoples may retain aspects of their cultural heritage to the extent that they wish, while at the same time both seeking to (and being free to) participate as fully as possibly in the life of the larger society.

With respect to behavioural shifts, (see Berry, 1980a for a review), there is now substantial evidence that there is variable change in peoples' daily activities during acculturation, depending on the behavioural domain and on the group. With respect to language, the Non-Official Languages Study nationally (O'Bryan et al, 1976) and numerous subsequent studies regionally (e.g. Breton et al, 1990) have shown that there is both large scale language maintenance and language loss. Similarly, identities and values, dress and food preferences, and many other daily behaviours change during acculturation. Most frequently these changes exhibit acquisition of behaviours that are similar to those that are characteristic of the larger society; but it is not always the case that there is a concomitant loss of behaviours characteristic of the heritage group (Berry, 1990a). That is, sometimes there is behavioural assimilation (involving heritage culture loss and larger society acquisition), and sometimes there is behavioural Integration (involving behaviours rooted in both cultural traditions) such as bilingualism, hyphenated-identities, and day-by-day behavioural switching according to immediate context and need. The implication of these kinds of behavioural changes is that the increased *similarity* (both cultural and psychological) between the groups in contact is likely to lead to greater mutual acceptance.

In contrast, where behaviours do not change very much (as is the case of those who are following the Separation strategy) the maintenance of a life style largely unaltered by living in Canada appears to be a source of negative attitudes and discrimination among members of the larger society. However, little direct evidence for this relationship is available, and is a candidate for urgent research. Similarly, the lack of responsive change among individual members and institutions of the larger society appears to be a major irritant for acculturating individuals and groups, especially for visible minorities. Once again, though, little empirical evidence (other than observations and anecdotes) is available on this point, and research is much needed.

The social and psychological characteristics of those who have become marginalized were previously described. Since these qualities are generally negatively-valued they are very likely to be irritants for members of the larger society, who often consider such persons and groups to be responsible for their own situation. Converting this "blaming the victim" attitude in the larger society into one that accepts major responsibility for what has taken place, is a precondition for improved intergroup relations. At the same time, such social and psychological problems have to become "owned" by the marginalized group, in the double sense of recognizing and accepting their existence ("owning up"), and in taking responsibility for bringing about change within their own communities. The experience in Canada with such marginalized 'situations and groups (for example, Metis and urban Native peoples, and Nova Scotia Blacks) should convince us of the importance of the issue; the essential test of Canada's ability to evolve equitable and tolerant human relations will be our capacity to solve extant marginalized situations, and to avoid developing other ones among newly-immigrating groups.

Acculturation, as we have seen, can often involve considerable stress; for this outcome the notion of *acculturative stress* has been developed. There is evidence (Berry, et al, 1987; 1997) that one's acculturation strategy is one important factor in such stress: those who feel Marginalized tend to be highly stressed, and those who maintain a Separation goal are also stressed; in contrast those who pursue Integration are minimally stressed, with Assimilation leading to intermediate levels. The phase of acculturation is also important: those in first contact, and those who have achieved some long term adaptation tend to be less stressed than those caught in the conflict or crisis phase, especially as we have noted, if they also feel marginalized.

Another factor is the way in which the host society exerts its acculturative influences. One important distinction is the degree of pluralism present in a society (Murphy, 1965). Culturally plural societies, in contrast to culturally monistic ones, are likely to be characterized by two important factors: one is the availability of a network of social and cultural groups which may provide support for those entering into the experience of acculturation; and the other is a greater tolerance for, or acceptance of, Cultural diversity (termed "multicultural ideology" by Berry, et al., 1977). One might reasonably expect the stress of persons experiencing acculturation in plural societies to be lower than those in monistic societies who pursue a forced inclusion or assimilationist ideology.

In assimilationist societies, there are a number of factors operating that will plausibly lead to greater acculturative stress than in pluralistic societies. If a person | regularly receives the message that one's culture, language and identity are unacceptable, the impact on one's sense of security and self-esteem will clearly be negative. If one is told that the price of admission to full participation in the larger society is to no longer be what one has grown up to be, the psychological conflict is surely heightened. And if, collectively, one's group is offered admission only on terms specified by the dominant society, then the potential for social conflict is also increased. Thus, assimilationist policies and actions on the part of the larger society can be plausibly linked to greater acculturative stress when compared to integrationist policies.

A related factor, paradoxically, is the existence of policies which are designed to *exclude* acculturating groups from full participation in the larger society though acts of discrimination, to the extent that acculturating people wish to participate in the desirable features of the larger society (such as adequate housing, medical care, political rights) the denial of these may be cause for increased levels of acculturative stress.

A final set of social variables refers to the acceptance or prestige of one's group in the acculturation setting. As we have seen, some groups are more acceptable on grounds of ethnicity, race, or religion than others; those less acceptable run into barriers (prejudice, discrimination, exclusion) which may lead to Marginalization of the group and which are likely to induce greater stress.

Beyond these social factors numerous psychological variables may play a role in the mental health status of persons experiencing acculturation. Here again a distinction is useful between those characteristics which were present prior to contact, and those which developed during acculturation. In the precontact set of variables are included certain experiences which may predispose one to function more effectively under acculturative pressures. These are: prior knowledge of the new language and culture, prior intercultural encounters of any kind, motives for the contact (voluntary vs. involuntary contact), and attitudes toward contact (positive or negative).

Contact experiences may also account for variations in acculturative stress. Whether one has a lot of contacts with the larger society (or few of them), whether they are pleasant (or unpleasant), whether they meet the current needs of the individual (or not), and in particular whether the first encounters are viewed positively (or not) may set the stage for all subsequent ones, and affect mental health.

Among factors which appear during acculturation are the various acculturation strategies: as noted in the previous section, individuals within a group do vary in their preference for Assimilating, Integrating or Separating. These variations, along with experiences of Marginalization, are known to affect one's mental health status (Berry et al., 1987).

The personal and societal outcomes of acculturative stress have been known for decades. At the personal level, reduced health (physical, social and psychological), lowered levels of motivation, a sense of alienation, and increased social deviance have been documented. At the societal level, there are direct counterparts in increased health costs, lower educational and work attainment (with related higher welfare costs), increased social conflict (intrafamilial and intergroup), substance abuse, criminal activity and a general societal malaise. Clearly, with these outcomes likely, policies that seek to avoid, or at least control, high levels of acculturative stress, are to be preferred.

Recent work (reviewed in Beiser et al, 1988) indicates that a desire to participate in the larger society, or a desire for cultural maintenance, if thwarted, can lead to a serious decline in the mental health status of acculturating individuals. Policies or attitudes in the larger society that are discriminatory (not permitting participation, and leading to Marginalization or Segregation) or assimilationist (leading to enforced cultural loss) are all predictors of psychological problems. In my view, acculturative stress is always a possible concomitant of acculturation, but its probability of occurrence can be much reduced if both participation in the larger society and maintenance of one's heritage culture are welcomed by policy and practice of the larger society.

Social Benefits and Costs of Multiculturalism

In this Section we draw upon the policy, context, theory and empirical findings outlined in the previous sections in order to estimate the social benefits and costs of operating a multicultural society. This analysis takes into account both the intended goals of multiculturalism, and the actual and possible outcomes that can be discerned in the materials reviewed.

The Canadian Multiculturalism Policy is clearly intended to manage intergroup and interpersonal relations in Canada by creating certain positive conditions for their improvement. The goal of this management is to support (even encourage) groups and individuals to adopt the Integration strategy (as defined in this paper), following a midcourse between the alternatives of Assimilation and Separation, and moving away from the social and psychological pathologies associated with Marginalization. While seeking to manage and encourage in these ways, the Policy also supports individual and group choice; the emphasis on human rights,. social participation and equity, as well as on group maintenance and intergroup tolerance demonstrates this concern with individual freedoms. In one sense, it is a balancing act between collective rights and individual rights: collective "life style" preferences should not constrain individual "life chances". In another sense, it is between two sets of collective rights - those of the dominant society and those of the various constituent groups. Value judgements regarding such pluralism and individualism (e.g. Bibby, 1990; Spicer 1991; Plant, 1991; Kymlicka, 1996) are now frequently in the public discourse about multiculturalism. Given the generally personal basis of such judgements, it is difficult to achieve any consensus about these issues. However, | now turn to a consideration of them based upon the evidence reviewed.

With respect to the Policy itself, there are two immediate benefits that likely result from its very existence without regard to whether it is "right" or "wrong". First it demonstrates our social concern for, and attention to the quality of human relations in Canada; the absence of a policy would presumably signal the opposite. It at least makes all people aware that their ethnocultural and individual needs are not being ignored; psychologically this may very well be a contributor to morale and self-esteem (which is one of the factors noted earlier that contribute to positive group relations). This benefit may be equally important for members of the larger society, since the multiculturalism policy exists for *all* Canadians.

Second, the policy can be construed as a "primary prevention" programme (cf Williams & Berry, 1991), in which known factors are used to foster positive relations and adaptations, rather than -waiting until problems appear. The intention is to give *every* individual and ethnocultural group (whether dominant or non-dominant) a place, a sense of belonging, in Canadian society; psychologically such a sense of place may again provide a boost to morale and self-esteem.

Beyond these two possible beneficial consequence of just having a multicultural policy, there are other general benefits that can be linked to its specific content. First is the general point of view that *diversity is* a *resource.* In biological systems theory, the greater the variance in a population, the greater is the capacity of that population to deal effectively with changing circumstances. A population that adapts completely to its habitat, by developing a homogeneous response to it, loses its range of alternatives. This view is captured by the adage: "adaptation is the enemy of adaptability". In social systems, homogeneity also reduces the ability of societies and institutions to respond to change, while diversity provides a range of choices.

Four specific instances of this general principle can be identified. In one, Canada's role as an international participant in diplomatic and political events can be enhanced by having a population in which cultural, linguistic, religious and value sensibilities can be found that match (and hence presumably understand) events in other societies. Our self-image as the international "good boy" is one that most Canadians appreciate, especially when travelling or working abroad, and has come to be a valued element in our definition of what it means to be Canadian. The maintenance of ethnocultural diversity at home may be seen as an important factor in our ability to participate abroad.

The second specific instance is more economic in character (but is closely linked to the first, so is mentioned here for completeness). In the initiative called "Multiculturalism Works", the Ministry has emphasized the international trade and domestic employment advantages of maintaining cultural and linguistic diversity in the Canadian population. Knowledge of variations in negotiating style, in subtle interpersonal relations (as well as a knowledge of the language) can be crucial to international economic relations. Such an extant resource in the Canadian population is a clear advantage especially for a country that lags in other competitive domains, such as productivity or research and development activity.

A third specific instance can be identified, this one at the individual level. If the Integration mode of acculturation resembles most closely the intention of the Multiculturalism policy, then personal diversity (in the sense of knowing how to live and work in two cultural worlds) gives a person flexibility and choice in daily life that those who have become assimilated or remain Separated do not have; and, of course, those who have become marginalized have the fewest choices of all.

The fourth specific instance is also at the individual level. Just as there seems to be no limit to the number of languages a person can master, there may well be no limit to the number of cultures an individual can acquire and appreciate. Since one of the goals of our formal educational system is to provide individuals with an enriched environment, it makes sense to provide this in a living environment, rather than just through books or other mediated experience.

The second general benefit of multiculturalism is that, in principle, it permits us to better meet our international *obligations with respect to human rights*. This benefit is rather intangible, but nevertheless important. The extent to which we have actually lived up to our potential is a matter of debate, one that is beyond the terms of reference of this Report. However, most would agree that there is room for improvement in many areas (Aboriginal Rights, national self-determination, culturally-sensitive health and education, and the reduction of bias in policing and the delivery of justice). The point is, that with the existence of multiculturalism policy and programmes, there is an ethical framework within which to work toward the improvement of human rights and social conditions in Canada. The alternatives imply the denial of the right to be different (Assimilation), the rejection of persons who pursue that right (Segregation) or both (Marginalization).

The third general benefit of multiculturalism is the potential for promoting the *social and psychological well being* of all Canadians. Using the framework presented in Figure 3, the potential benefits of the Integration option have to be judged in relation to the potential costs of the alternatives. The argument is that Integration promotes the social and psychological well being of all Canadians, while Segregation, Separation, Assimilation and Marginalization reduces them, even for the dominant society.

To begin, I assume that there is no support for a Segregation policy: inevitable problems with international diplomacy, trade and human rights (the benefits just mentioned) would not likely be accepted by Canadians, quite apart from the psychological and social problems that such a policy would entail (Lambley, 1980: W.H.O., 1983). Similarly, while Separation is possible (since national self determination is generally considered to be a basic collective human right), the social conflict and psychological stress associated with this option renders it less than attractive for most individuals and groups in Canada. Indeed, all ethnocultural associations, and all Aboriginal groups who seek an enhanced place for themselves do so with an explicit commitment to achieving it within Confederation. Conclude that, whatever changes may take place in the direction of greater ethnocultural distinctiveness, they are unlikely to entail either Segregation or Separation as their eventual outcomes.

The second alternative, that of Assimilation has sometimes been promoted on the grounds that the elimination of group differences will lead to the elimination of the basis for social conflict. Two direct arguments are available to counter this position. One is that in contemporary societies that have pursued assimilationist policies (e.g. the U.S. : "E Pluribus Unum", and France : "Unité de l'Hexagon"), group differences have obviously not been reduced or even disappeared. Black, Hispanic and Asian cultures have persisted in the U.S., as have regional cultures (e.g. Breton, Basque, Catalan) in France. Indeed, both countries have had to make recent changes in their assimilationist stances : bilingual education in the U.S., and bilingual signs (French-Breton) in France. It is also plausible to relate high levels of overt intergroup conflict (e.g. black-white, Basque-French), and possibly similar levels of social deviance to the struggle over the right to be culturally different in assimilationist societies.

A second direct argument is psychological : individuals, even in homogeneous groups, seek to differentiate themselves one from another, even to the extent of establishing two or more distinct groups within the original population. The work of Tajfel (1978, 1982) has clearly demonstrated this phenomenon. Self distinctiveness, leading to group distinctiveness, seems to be a fundamental psychological process, where there is a tendency to converge, there is also a tendency to diverge. The implication of this phenomenon of differentiation is that assimilationist activity is likely to be countered by differentiation activity, leading to a nullification of such a policy initiative. Assimilation is thus not only difficult to achieve, but appears to run counter to a fundamental psychological process.

The third alternative, that of Marginalization, has already been described as an outcome fraught with social and psychological pathologies. For example, among Aboriginal peoples in the Arctic (e.g. Berry, 1990b) six indicators of social and mental malaise. (suicide, homicide, spousal and child abuse, and alcohol and drug abuse) along with other social indicators (e.g. incarceration) reveal an epidemic of major proportions. Most observers attribute this situation, not to qualities of Aboriginal peoples, or to the larger society, but to the character of the relationships between them; this is easily identified as a classic case of Marginalization of Aboriginal peoples by the larger society. The danger of such an outcome befalling other groups is always present, and clearly must be avoided at all costs.

The Integration option, the one that most closely resembles the main features of Multiculturalism policy in Canada, is thus to be preferred on the basis of the costs associated with the alternatives. However, a strong positive case can be made for Integration on its own merits. We have already noted that confidence and a sense of place are likely to be the outcomes of the policy for both dominant and non-dominant groups: In both the intergroup relations and the acculturation literatures, increased potential for security and tolerance, and reduced potential for stress were shown to flow from the Integrationist strategy. These demonstrable empirical relationships provide the most direct evidence for the social and psychological benefits of multiculturalism to be found in the literature; they are apparently robust and reliable, and will likely stand the test of future investigation.

Turning to the possible costs of *Multiculturalism*, there are three distinct arguments that have been advanced. First is an *"economic"* cost. the dollars needed to operate a host of programmes related to the support of cultural and linguistic maintenance, of contact and participation, and of various forms of equity. Most recently this argument has been heard with respect to bilingualism in Ontario ("The French Languages Services Act"), but has been also heard with respect to immigration, refugees, pay and employment equity. On the basis of research on one of these issues with one involved group (Berry & Bourcier, 1989), my conclusion is that the "economic" argument is merely an attempt to put a rational front on deepseated underlying bigotry. In terms used earlier, the economic argument is a "subtle" or "symbolic" form of prejudice, and deserves to be recognized as such.

A second possible cost lies in the potential for *ethnic and racial discrimination and inequality*. encouraging people to remain different makes them easy targets for such action. As noted earlier, the existence. of the "Vertical Mosaic" was initially claimed to be evidence of discrimination resulting in inequality among ethnic and racial groups. However, Pineo and Porter (1985) subsequently considered there to be evidence for the "collapse of the vertical mosaic". In a study of educational achievement in Toronto, Richmond (1988) found that while ethnicity was a relatively important factor in determining how far one went in school, second generation non-British achieved more educational upward mobility than did the second generation British.

Most recently, Breton et al. (1990) concluded that there is no general relationship between ethnicity and status : participation varies by ethnic group and by domains (economic, political and social); sometimes ethnicity is a hindrance, but sometimes it is an asset to full participation in the larger society. Of course, the presence of variability in this phenomenon means that some individuals in some groups in some situations will be the targets of prejudice and discrimination; and most would agree that this is unacceptable in a society that pursues tolerance as a general goal. However, the culprit is more likely to be specific attitudes toward specific groups in specific circumstances, rather than the general policy of multiculturalism. What is needed is a concerted attack on these instances, rather than attacking the policy as a whole.

Indeed, the current first priority of the Ministry of Multiculturalism and Citizenship is Race Relations, in apparent recognition of where the specific problems lie. The evidence presented earlier clearly shows that it is those of non-European background in Canada who are most negatively evaluated, who are least prestigious, and who are most discriminated against. Alternative explanations are possible (rooted in some possible correlates of "race", such as perceived similarity, familiarity, accent, values); these need to be examined systematically before the source of the rejection can be unambiguously identified and the specific root causes dealt with. However, such needed research should not delay the implementation of programmes to reduce the overt discrimination apparent in Canada at the present time.

A third cost is the potential for increased *divisiveness and a reduction of national unity*. In an earlier analysis (Kalin & Berry, 1982b) we concluded that there is no necessary conflict between multiculturalism and achieving national unity. Further, evidence from the 1991 survey (Kalin & Berry, 1995) shows that prefering an ethnic or hyphenated identity (over a civic one) in no way diminishes an individuals sense of attachment or commitment to the larger society that is Canada. The evidence reviewed suggests that generally, Canadians are moderately tolerant of diversity, and accepting of multiculturalism; there appears to be no serious personal conflict for those who think of themselves as both Canadian and as a member of a particular ethnocultural group; and there appears to be no serious ethnic or regional conflict that is about to take the form of overt and sustained violence that periodically afflict other plural societies (Reitz, 1988). If anything, these threats to national unity may be diminished, rather than enhanced, by the multiculturalism policy, giving each individual and group at least some place in an overall national, heterogeneous society.

Other possible costs have been alluded to in the earlier discussions. In the section on Immigration, the increasing settlement of visible minorities in the metropolitan centres of Montreal, Toronto, Calgary and Vancouver was noted, but there is no current evidence of a "tipping point" in Canada. In contrast, popular wisdom frequently assumes that urban concentrations of visible minorities are problematic.

Beyond this lack of evidence for a tipping point, we can also rely upon theoretical positions. On the one hand, urban concentrations provide "targets"; but on the other, they provide "support groups". On the one hand they may enhance "cultural maintenance"; but on the other, they may inhibit "contact and participation". On the one hand they may generate feelings of threat and insecurity for members of the larger society; but on the other, they may create a sense of security and self-esteem for members of the particular groups. We must conclude that on theoretical grounds, there is a stalemate. The one clear statement that is possible is that both empirical and theoretical work is urgently needed in order to decide the issue.

Another possible cost alluded to earlier is how easily the larger society can adapt to the changing social reality in Canada. Both the demography and the policy responses are changing rapidly, and many apparently feel that the speed is too great and the distance too far (see Spicer, 1991 for evidence of such views). Evidence was presented earlier indicating that those who are relatively older, who are less well-educated, and who have had few intercultural contacts during their lives, are likely to feel threatened by these changes. Aware of current norms about the overt expression of prejudice, many assert their views in economic ("costly"; "job loss"), or social ("race riots"; "lower quality of education") terms. While recent research (e.g., Berry & Kalin, 1995) shows these assertions to be invalid, these views are important Statements of legitimate underlying concerns by members of Canadian society. If treated as such, and if steps are taken to reduce the perception of threat, the potential costs will not likely materialize. However, if ignored or ridiculed, feelings of threat may well be exacerbated, and potential costs will become converted into substantial ones through organized backlash and reaction.

On balance, the benefits of multiculturalism appear to vastly outweigh the costs at the present time. This is partly due to the essential validity of some of the elements of the policy, and partly due to a process of continuing refinement of programmes that have been developed to implement the policy. For example, the change in emphasis in the mid 1970's toward 'contact and participation, and away from group maintenance (sometimes called the shift from "cultural" to "social" priorities), probably reduced the potential for increased ethnocentrism. And the more recent shift toward improving race relations as a key to managing Canada's diversity signals an awareness of the likely major source of social conflict.

The only possible alternative to Multiculturalism (Assimilation) has not been Successful elsewhere in the world, and would likely be massively resisted if tried in Canada (leading to levels of social conflict not previously encountered here). In any case, having announced ourself to the world for two decades as Officially multicultural, we are not likely to get away with changing the rules for those who perhaps came for this very reason. Moreover, it would be difficult to justify the differential treatment of British, French and Aboriginal peoples (who clearly would not accept Assimilation of one group to another), and those groups who are less well placed demographically or politically in Canadian society.

In conclusion, it appears that the only viable and realistic course is to pursue the Integration option, guided by the policy of Multiculturalism.

Implications for Immigration and Multiculturalism Policy

Based on the theoretical and empirical literature, and on the consideration of benefits and costs, my judgement is that there need be no substantial changes in Multiculturalism policy in Canada at the present time. The psychological conditions that underlie the successful operation of a multicultural society are well-articulated in the multiculturalism policy, and are generally being implemented by the various programmes. There are: *providing a sense of cultural security for all who wish to maintain a degree of cultural distinctiveness*, and at the same time *providing opportunities for all* to *participate equitably in the economic and political life of this country*. In principle, there should be no cost to this joint pursuit (in terms of sacrificing one in order to achieve the other); and there can be substantial benefit to pursuing both simultaneously. If these are accomplished, then the third and ultimate policy goal is achievable: *the attainment of a tolerant population, in which there is cultural space and mutual acceptance by all sectors of the Canadian population.*

It has been a pleasure to share these ideas and findings with you. This view from Canada may or may not make sense to those attempting to manage pluralism in India. As a cross-cultural researcher, I am well aware that psychological findings rooted in the concepts and data from one culture cannot be assumed to apply in other cultures. This overview is offered to stimulate parallel research, and if appropriate, research with new conceptualizations that may well challenge the views expressed in these lectures.

References

Aboud, F., & Skerry, S. (1984). The development of ethnic attitudes: a critical review. *Joumal of Cross-Cultural Psychology,* 15, 3-34.

Aldwin, C. (1994). *Stress, coping and development.* New York: Guilford Press.

Amir, Y. (1976). The role of intergroup contact in change of prejudice and ethnic relations. In P. Katz (Ed.), *Towards the elimination of racism.* New York: Pergamon.

Aronowitz, M. (1992). Adjustment of immigrant children as a function of parental attitudes to change. *International Migration Review*, 26, 86-110.

Aycan, Z. & Berry, J.W. (1994). Impact of economic factors on immigrants psychological well-being and adaptation. Paper presented at 12th *International Congress of Cross-Cultural Psychology*, Pamplona.

Aycan, Z. & Berry, J.W. (1995). Cross-cultural adaptation as a multifaceted phenomenon. Paper presented at 4th *European Congress of Psychology*, Athens.

Bagley, C. (1979). Self-esteem as a pivotal concept in race and ethnic relations. *Research in Race and Ethnic Relations*, I, |27-|67.

Balakrishnan, T.R. (1988). *Immigration and the changing ethnic mosaic of Canadian cities.* Report submitted to the Demographic Review, Government of Canada (1989). *Charting Canada's future: A report of the demographic Review.* Ottawa: Supply and Services.

Beiser M., Johnson, P. & Turner, J. (1993). Unemployment, underemployment and depressive affect among southeast Asian refugees. *Psychological Medicine*, 23, 731-743.

Beiser, M., Barwick, C., Berry, J.W., da Costa, G., Fantino, A., Ganesan, S. Lee, C., Milne, W., Naidoo, J., Prince, R. Tousignant, M., & Vela, E. (1988). *After the door has been opened: Mental health issues affecting immigrants and refugees.* (Report of the Federal Taskforce on Mental Health Issues Affecting Immigrants and Refugees). Ottawa: Ministry of Health and Welfare, and Ministry of Multiculturalism and Citizenship.

Beiser, M. R, M., Johnson, P. & Turner, J. (1993). Unemployment, underemployment and depressive affect among Southeast Asian refugees. *Psychological Medicine*, 23, 731-743.

Berry, J.W. (1970). Marginality, stress and ethnic identification in an acculturated Aboriginal community. *Journal of Cross-Cultural Psychology*, 1: 239-252.

Berry, J.W. (1974). Psychological aspects of cultural pluralism: Unity and identity reconsidered. *Topics in Culture Leaming*, 2, 17-22.

Berry, J.W. (1976). *Human Ecology and Cognitive Style: Comparative Studies in Cultural and Psychological Adaptation.* New York: Sage/Halsted.

Berry, J.W. (1980a). Social and cultural change. In H.C. Triandis and R. Brislin (Eds). *Handbook of cross-cultural psychology*, (*Volume 5, Social psychology*). Boston: Allyn & Bacon.

Berry, J.W. (I980b) Native peoples and the larger society. In R. Gardner & R. Kalin (Eds.) *A Canadian social psychology of ethnic relations.* Toronto: Methuen.

Berry, J.W. (1984a). Multicultural policy in Canada: A social psychological analysis. *Canadian Joumal of Behavioural Science*, 16, 353-370.

Berry, J.W. (1984b). Cultural relations in plural societies: Alternatives to segregation and their socio-psychological implications. In N. Miller & M.B. Brewer (Eds.), *Groups in contact*, (pp. 11-27). New York: Academic Press.

Berry, J.W. (1985). Cultural psychology and ethnic psychology: A comparative analysis. In I. Reyes-Lagunes and Y. Poortinga (Eds.), *From a different perspective.* Amsterdam: Swets & Zeitlinger.

Berry, J.W. (1990a) Psychology of Acculturation. In R. Brislin (Ed.) *Applied Cross-Cultural Psychology.* London: Sage.

Berry, J.W. (1990b) *Body and Soul: Physical, social and psychological health contrasts among Abonginal Peoples in Canada, Greenland and Alaska.* Paper presented to Circumpolar Health Congress, Yukon.

Berry, J.W. (1991). Understanding and managing multiculturalism. *Joumal of Psychology and Developing Societies*, 3, 17-49.

Berry, J.W. (1992). Acculturation and adaptation in a new society. *Intemational Migration*, 30, 69-85.

Berry, J.W. (1996). Individual and group relations in plural societies. In C. Granrose & S. Oskamp (Eds). *Cross-cultural workgroups*, (pp. 17-35). Thousand Oaks: Sage.

Berry, J.W. (1997). Immigration, acculturation and adaptation. *Applied Psychology*, 46, 5-68.

Berry, J.W. & Annis, R.C. (Eds.) (1988). *Ethnic psychology: research and practice with immigrants, refugees, ethnic groups, Native peoples and sojoumers.* Lisse. Swets & Zeitlinger.

Berry, J.W. & Bourcier, D. (1989) *Altitudes toward Official bilingualism.in Eastem Ontario.* Paper presented at Canadian Psychological Association Meetings, Halifax.

Berry, J.W., & Kalin, R. (1979). Reciprocity of inter-ethnic attitudes in a multicultural society. *International Joumal of Intercultural Relations*, 3, 99-112.

Berry, J.W. & Kalin, R. (1989). Unpublished Report to Ministry of Multiculturalism and Citizenship.

Berry, J.W. & Kalin, R. (1995). Multicultural and ethnic attitudes in Canada. *Canadian Joumal of Behavioural Science*, 27, 301-320.

Berry, J.W., Kalin, R. & Taylor, D. (1977). *Multiculturalism and ethnic attitudes in Canada.* Ottawa: Ministry of Supply and Services.

Berry, J. W., & Kim, U. (1988). Acculturation and mental health. In P. R. Dasen, J. W. Berry., & N. Sartorius (Eds.), *Health and Cross-cultural psychology: Towards applications* (pp. 207-238). Newbury Park: Sage.

Berry, J.W., Kim, U., Minde, T. & Mok, D. (1987). Comparative studies of acculturative stress. *International Migration Review*, 21, 491-511.

Berry, J.W., Kim, U., Power, S., & Bujaki, M. (1989). Acculturation attitudes in plural societies. *Applied Psychology*, 38, 185-206.

Berry, J.W. & Kostovcik, N. (1990). Psychological adaptation of Malaysian students in Canada. In AH. Othman & W.R.A. Rahman (Eds). *Psychology and Socio-Economic Development*, (pp. 155-162). Bangi: Penerbit Universiti Kebangsaan Malaysia.

Berry, J.W. & Laponce, J. (Eds.) (1994). *Ethnicity and culture.in Canada: The research landscape.* Toronto: University of Toronto Press.

Berry, J.W., Poortinga, Y.H., Pandey, J., Dasen, P.R., Saraswathi, T.S., Segall, M.H. & Kagitcibasi, C. (Eds). *Handbook of Cross-Cultural Psychology* (3 Vols). Boston: Allyn & Bacon.

Berry, J.W., Poortinga, Y.H., Segall, M.H. & Dasen, P.R. (1992). *Cross-Cultural Psychology: Research and Applications.* New York: Cambridge University Press.

Berry, J.W. & Sam, D. (1997). Acculturation and adaptation. In J.W. Berry, M.H. Segall & Kagitcibasi (Eds). *Handbook of cross-cultural psychology.* Vol. 3, Social behavior and applications. Boston: Allyn & Bacon.

Berry, JW. & Wells, M. (1994). Attitudes toward Aboriginal peoples and Aboriginal self-government in Canada. In J. Hylton (Ed.) *Aboriginal peoples and Aboriginal self-govemment in Canada*, (pp. 215-232). Saskatoon: Purich Publishing.

Bibby, R. (1990). *Mosaic madness.* Toronto: Stoddart.

Bibby, R. (1987). Bilingualism and Multiculturalism: A national reading. In L. Driedger (Ed). *Ethnic Canada: Identities and inequalities*, Toronto: Copp Clark Pitman. Bisoondath, N. (1993). Myths and Multiculturalism, Toronto: McClelland & Stewart.

Bourhis, R. (1994). Ethnic and language attitudes in Quebec. In J.W. Berry & J. Laponce (Eds). *Ethnicity and culture in Canada: The research landscape.* (pp. 322-360). Toronto: University of Toronto Press.

Boyd, M., Goyden, J., Jones, F., McRoberts, H., Pineo, P. & Porter, J. (1981). Status attainment in Canada: Findings of the Canadian mobility study. *Canadian Review of Sociology and Anthropology*, 18, 657-673.

Breton, R., Reitz, J.G. & Valentine, V. (1980). *Cultural Boundaries and the cohesion of Canada.* Montreal: Institute for Research on Futlic Policy.

Breton, R., Isajiw, W., Kalbach, W. & Reitz, J. (1990). *Ethnic identity and equality.* Toronto: University of Toronto Press.

Brewer, M., & Campbell, D.T. (1976). *Ethnocentrism and intergroup attitudes: East African evidence.* New York: Sage/Halsted.

Burnet, J. (1978). The policy of multiculturalism within a bilingual framework: a stocktaking. *Canadian Ethnic Studies*, 10, 107-113.

Burnet, J. (1979). Myths and multiculturalism. *Canadian Joumal of Education*, 4, 43-58.

Burnet, J. (1975). The policy of multiculturalism within a bilingual framework: an interpretation. In A. Wolfgang (Ed.), *Education of immigrant students.* Toronto: OISE.

Cameron, J. & Berry, J.W. (1990). *Intergroup attitudes: self-esteem and threats to identity.* Paper presented at Canadian Psychological Association Meetings, Ottawa.

Cameron, J. & Lalonde, R. (1994). Self, ethnicity and social group memberships in two generations of Italian Canadians. *Personality and Social Psychology Bulletin*, 20, 514-520.

Carlin, J. (1990). Refugee and immigrant populations at special risk: Women, children and the elderly. In W.H. Holtzman & T. Bornemann (Eds.) *Mental Health of Immigrants and Refugees.* Austin: Hogg Foundation for Mental Health.

Church, A. (1982). Sojourner adjustment. *Psychological Bulletin*, 91, 540-572.

Cumming, P., Lee, E. & Oreopoulos, D. (1989). *Access to Trades and Professions.* Toronto: Ontario Ministry of Citizenship.

Diaz-guerrero, R. (1979). The development of coping style. *Human Development*, 22, 320-331.

Dion, K. (1989). *Ethnicity and perceived discrimination : A comparative survey of six ethnic groups in Toronto.* Paper presented to Canadian Ethnic Studies Conference, Calgary.

Dion K. (1985). Social distance norms in Canada: Effects of stimulus characteristics and dogmatism. *Intemational Journal of Psychology*, 20, 743-749.

Driedger, L. (1989). *The ethnic factor: Identity in diversity.* Toronto : McGraw-Hill Ryerson.

Duckitt, J. (1992). *The social psychology of prejudice.* New York : Praeger.

Endler, N. & Parker, J. (1990). Multidimensional assessment of coping. *Journal of Personality and Social Psychology*, 58, 844-854.

Esses, V., Jackson, L., Nolan, J. & Armstrong, T. (1997). Economic threat and attitudes towards immigrants. In S. Halli & L. Driedger (Eds.), *Immigrant Canada.* Toronto : University of Toronto Press.

Fenton, C. (1989). Racism and mental health. In J. Cox & S. Bostock (Eds). *Racial discrimination in health services.* Keele : University Press.

Fernando, S. (1993). Racism and xenophobia. *Innovation in Social Sciences Research* (Special Issue on Migration and Health), 6, 9-19.

Frese, M. (1986). Coping as a moderator and mediator between stress at work and psychosomatic complaints. In M.H. Appley, & R. Trumbull (Eds), *Dynamics of stress*, (pp. 183-206). New York: Plenum.

Frye, N. (1971). *The bush garden.* Toronto: Anansi.

Ghuman, P. A. S. (1991). Best or worst of two worlds? A study of Asian adolescents. *Educational Review*, 33, 121-132.

Goodenough, W. H. (1976). Multiculturalism as the normal human experience. *Anthropology and Education Quarterly*, 7, 4-7.

Government of Canada (1971). Statement to the House by the Prime Minister, October 8, I97I, in response to the recomniendations of the Royal Commission on Bilingualism and Biculturalism, Book IV, *The Cultural Contribution of the Other Ethnic Groups.*

Government of Canada (1989). Charting Canada's future : *A report of the demographic Review.* Ottawa; Ministry of Supply and Services.

Government of Canada (1989) *Multiculturalism Policy and Programmes.* Ottawa: Multiculturalism and Citizenship.

Government of Canada (1988) *Bill C-93: An Act for the Preservation and Enhancement of Multiculturalism in Canada.* Ottawa : Parliament of Canada.

Graves, T. (967). Psychological acculturation in a tri-ethnic community, *South-westem Joumal of Anthropology*, 23, 337-350.

Hagendoorn, L. (1993). Ethnic categorization and outgroup exclusion: The role of cultural values and social stereotypes in the construction of ethnic hierarchies. *Ethnic and Racial Studies*, 16, 26-51.

Halpern, D. (1993). Minorities and mental health. *Social Science and Medicine*, 36, 597-607.

Hauff, E. & Vaglum, P. (1993). Integration of Vietnamese refugees into the Norweigian Labour Market : The impact of war trauma. *Intemational Migration Review*, 27, 388-405

Henry, F. & Ginsberg, E. (1985). Who Gets the Work? *A Test of Racial Discrimination in Employment.* Report to Urban Alliance on Race Relations, Toronto.

Henry, F. (1989). *Who Gets the Work in 1989*? Unpublished Report submitted to Economic Council of Canada.

Ho, E. (1995). *The challenge of culture change : The cross-cultural adaptation of Hong Kong Chinese adolescent immigrants in New Zealand.* Unpublished Doctoral Thesis, University of Waikato, New Zealand.

Jayasuriya, L., Sang, D. & Fielding, A. (1992). *Ethnicity, immigration and mental illness: A critical review of Australian research.* Canberra: Bureau of Immigration Research.

Kalin, R. (1981). Ethnic attitudes. In R.C. Gardner & R. Kalin (Eds.), *A Canadian social psychology of ethnic relations.* Toronto : Methuen.

Kalin, R. (1996). Ethnic attitudes as a function of ethnic presence. *Canadian Journal of Behavioural Science*, 28, 171-179.

Kalin, R. & Berry, J.W. (1982a). The social ecology of ethnic attitudes in Canada. *Canadian Journal of Behavioural Science*, 14, 97-109.

Kalin, R. & Berry, J.W. (1982b). Canadian ethnic attitudes and identity in the context of national unity. *Journal of Canadian Studies*, 17, 103-110.

Kalin R. & Berry, J.W. (1994). Ethnic and multicultural attitudes in Canada outside Québec. In J.W. Berry & J. Laponce (Eds), *Ethnicity and culture in Canada: The Research Landscape.* Toronto: University of Toronto Press.

Kalin R. & Berry, J.W. (1995). Ethnic and civic self-identity in Canada. *Canadian Ethnic Studies.* 27, 1-15.

Kalin, R. & Berry, J.W. (1996). Interethnic attitudes in Canada: Ethnocentrism, consensual hierarchy and reciprocity. *Canadian Journal of behavioural Science*, 28, 253-261.

Kealey, D. J. (1989). A study of cross-cultural effectiveness: Theoretical issues, practical applications. *International Journal of Intercultural Relations*, 13, 387-428.

Krishnan, A., & Berry, J. W. (1992). Acculturative stress and acculturation attitudes among Indian immigrants to the United States. *Psychology and Developing Societies*, 4, 187-212.

Kymlicka, W. (1995). *Multicultural citizenship.* Oxford: Clarendon Press.

LaFromboise, T., Coleman, H. & Gerton, J. (1993). Psychological impact of biculturalism: Evidence and theory. *Psychological Bulletin*, 114, 395-412.

Lalonde, R. & Cameron, J. (1993). An intergroup perspective on immigrant acculturation with a focus on collective strategies. *International Journal of Psychology*, 28, 57-74.

Lambert, N.E., Mermegis, L. & Taylor, D.M. (1986). Greek Canadians' attitudes towards own group and other Canadian ethnic groups : A test of the multiculturalism hypothesis. *Canadian Journal of Behavioural Science*, 18, 35-51.

Lambley, P. (1980). *The psychology of apartheid. Athens* : University of Georgia press.

Lazarus, R. S. (1990). Theory-based stress measurement. *Psychological Inquiry*, 1, 3-13.

Lazarus, R.S. (1991). The Psychological stress in the workplace. *Journal of Social Behavior and Personality*, 6, 1-13.

Lazarus, R.S. (1993). From psychological stress to the emotions: A history of changing outlooks. *Annual Review of Psychology*, 44, 1-21.

Lazarus, R.S. & Folkman, S. (1984). *Stress, appraisal and coping.* New York: Springer.

LeVine, R.A. & Campbell, D.T. (1972). *Ethnocentrism: Theories of conflict, ethnic attitudes and group behaviour.* New York : Wiley.

Lupul, M. (1989). Networking, discrimination and multiculturalism as a social philosophy. *Canadian Ethnic Studies*, 2, 1-12.

Moghaddam, F.M. (1988). Individualistic and collective integration strategies among immigrants. In J.W. Berry & R.C. Annis (Eds), *Ethnic psychology* (pp. 69-79). Amsterdam - Swets & Zeitlinger.

Moghaddam, F.M., Ditto, B & Taylor, D. (1990). Attitudes and attributions related to "symptomatology in Indian immigrant women. *Joumal of Cross-Cultural Psychology*, 21, 335-350.

Moghaddam, F.M. & Taylor, D.M. (1987). The meaning of multiculturalism for visible minority immigrant women. *Canadian Joumal of Behavioural Science*, 19, 121-136.

Moghaddam, F.M., Taylor, D.M., & Lalonde, R.N. (1989). Integration strategies and attitudes toward the built environment: A study of Haitian and Indian immigrant women in Montreal. *Canadian Journal of Behavioural Science*, 21, 160-173.

Murphy, H.B.M. (1965). Migration and the major mental disorders. In M.B. Kantor (Ed.). *Migration and mental health*. Springfield : Thomas.

Naidoo, J.C. (1992). The mental health of visible ethnic minorities in Canada. *Psychology and Developing Societies*, 4, 165-186.

Naidoo, J., & Davis, J.C. (1988). Canadian South Asian women in transition: A dualistic view of life. *Joumal of Comparative Family Studies*, 19, 311-327.

O'Bryan, K., Reitz, J., & Kuplowska, O. (1976). *Non-official languages*. Ottawa: Ministry of Supply and Services.

Palmer, H. (1975). *Immigration and the rise of multiculturalism*. Toronto: Copp Clark.

Passaris, C. (1987). Canada's demographic outlook and multicultural immigration. *Intemational Migration*, 25, 361-384.

Phinney, J. (1990). Ethnic identity in adolescents and adults: A review of research. *Psychological Bulletin*, 108, 499-514.

Pineo, P. (1977). The social standing of ethnic and racial groupings. *Canadian Review of Sociology and Anthropology*, l4, 147-157.

Pineo, P.C. & Porter, J. (1985). Ethnic origin and occupational attainment. In M. Boyd (Ed). *Ascription and achievement in Canada*. Ottawa : Carleton University Press.

Plant, G. (1991). Protecting the seeds of a new tomorrow. *Globe and Mail*, September 2.

Porter, J. (1972). Dilemmas and contradictions of a multiethnic society. *Transactions of the Royal Society of Canada*. 10, 193-205.

Porter, J. (1975). Ethnic pluralism in Canadian perspective. In N. Glazer & D. Moynihan (Eds.), *Ethnicity: Theory and experience*. Cambridge, Mass : Harvard University Press.

Redfield, R., Linton, R., Herskovits, M.J. (1936). Memorandum on the study of acculturation. *Amencan Anthropologist*, 38, 149-152.

Reitz, J. (1988). Less racial discrimination in Canada, or simply less racial conflict? *Canadian Public Policy*, 14, 424-44].

Richmond, A. (1986). Ethnogenerational variation in educational achievement. *Canadian Ethnic Studies*, 18, 75-89.

Richmond, A. (1988). *Immigration and ethnic conflict*. Toronto: MacMillan.

Richmond, A. (1993). Reactive migration: Sociological perspectives on refugee movements. *Journal of Refugee Studies*, 6, 7-24.

Roberts, L.W. & Clifton, R.A. (1982). Exploring the ideology of Canadian multiculturalism. *Canadian Public Policy*, 8, 88-94.

Sabatier, C. & Berry, J.W. (1994). Immigration et acculturation. In. R. Bourhis & J-P. Leyens (Eds). *Stéréotypes, discrimination et relations intergroupes*. Liege: Mardaga.

Sam, D. L. & Berry, J. W. (1995). Acculturative stress among young immigrants in Norway. *Scandinavian Joumal of Psychology*., 36, 10-24.

Samuda, R., Chodzinski, R., Berry, J.W. & Lewis, J. (1989). *Educational and Occupational Aspirations of Secondary School Students in Relation to Ethnic Group Membership.* Report submitted to Ministry of Multiculturalism.

Samuel, T.J. (1988). Immigration and visible minorities in the year 200I: A projection. *Canadian Ethnic Studies*. 20, 92-100.

Schmitz, P. (1992a). Immigrant mental and physical health. *Psychology and Developing Societies*, 4, 117-131.

Schmitz, P. (1992b). Acculturation styles and health. In S. lwawaki, Y. Kashima and K. Leung (Eds). *Innovations in Cross-Cultural Psychology*, Amsterdam: Swets and Zeitlinger.

Schmitz, P. G. (1994). Acculturation and adaptation process among immigrants in Germany. In A-M. Bouvy, F. J. R. van de Vijver, & P. Schmitz (Eds.), *Joumeys into cross-cultural psychology*. (pp. 142-157). Amsterdam: Swets & Zeitlinger.

Stonequist, E.V. (1937). *The marginal man*. New York: Scribner.

Szapocznik, J. & Kurtines, W. (1993). Family psychology and cultural diversity. *American Psychologist*, 48, 400-407.

Gordon, M.M. (1964). *Assimilation in American life*. New York: Oxford University Press.

Tajfel, H. (1978). *Differentiation between social groups*. London: Academic Press.

Tajfel, H. (1982). *Social identity and intergroup relations*. New York: Cambridge University Press.

Thorburn, H. (1989). The political foundations of Canada's pluralistic society. In O.P. Dwivendi (Ed). *Canada 2000. Race Relations and Public Policy*. Guelph: University of Guelph.

Triandis, H.C. (1976). The future of pluralism. *Joumal of Social Issues*, 32, 179-208.

UNESCO (1985). *Cultural pluralism and cultural identity*. Paris: UNESCO.

Ward, C. (1996). Acculturation. In D. Landis & R. Bhagat (Eds), *Handbook of Intercultural Training* (2nd Edition). Newbury Park: Sage.

Ward C. & Kennedy, A. (1992). Locus of control, mood disturbance and social difficulty during cross-cultural transitions. *Intemational Joumal of Intercultural Relations*, 16, 175-194.

Ward, C. & Kennedy, A. (1993a). Psychological and sociocultural adjustmentduring cross-cultural transitions: A comparison of secondary students overseas and at home. *International Joumal of Psychology*, 28, 129-147.

Ward, C., & Kennedy, A. (1993b). Where's the "culture" in cross-cultural transition? Comparative studies of sojourner adjustment. *Joumal of Cross-Cultural Psychology*, 24, 221-249.

Ward, 'C. & Kennedy, A. (1995). Crossing cultures: The relationship between psychological and sociocultural dimensions of cross-cultural adjustment. In J. Pandey, D. Sinha & P. Bhawuk (Eds). *Asian contributions to cross-cultural psychology*. New Delhi: Sage.

Ward C. & Searle, W. (1991). The impact of value discrepancies and cultural identity on psychological and sociocultural adjustment of sojourners. *Intemational Journal of Intercultural Relations*, 15, 209-225.

Williams, C. & Berry, J.W. (1991). Primary prevention of acculturative stress among refugees: the application of psychological theory and practice. *American Psychologist*, 46, 632-641.

Zheng, X., & Berry, J. W. (1991). Psychological adaptation of Chinese sojourners in Canada. *Intemational Journal of Psychology*, 26, 451-470.

World Health Organization (1983). *Apartheid and health*. Geneva: WHO.

Berry, J.W. (2003). Conceptual approaches to acculturation. In K. Chung, P. Balls-Organista& G. Marin (Eds.). Acculturation: Advances in Theory, Measurement, and Applied Research, (pp. 17-37). Washington: APA.

Berry, J.W. (Ed.) (2017).Mutual intercultural relations. Cambridge: Cambridge University Press.

Berry, J.W. (2019). Acculturation: A personal journey across cultures. Cambridge: Cambridge University Press/

Sam, D. L. & Berry, J.W. (2016) (Eds). Cambridge handbook of acculturation psychology) 2nd edition). Cambridge: Cambridge University Press.

Introduction of Authors

1. **Kalpana Kannabiran** is a Professor of Sociology and Regional Director of Council for Social Development, Hyderabad. Her research work is based on understanding the social foundations of non-discrimination, violence against women and questions of constitutionalism and social justice in India.

2. **Shaibal Gupta** is a Social Scientist. He is the best known expert on the politics & economics of Bihar. His research focuses on the structure of the Bihar Economy as well as on Nations Development issues in Bihar. He is an Economist by Profession. He has done.

3. **John W. Berry** is a Professor emeritus of Psychology at Queen's University, Kingston. He is a Ph. D. from the University of Edinburg. He has been a lecturer at the University of Sydney for three years, a Fellow of Netherlands Institute for Advanced Study and a visiting Professor at the University De Geneva. He is a past Secretary-General, past President and Honorary Fellow of the International Association for Cross- Cultural Psychology. He is the author or editor of over twenty books in the areas of cross- cultural, social and cognitive psychology.

Introduction of Editors

Dr. Badri Narayan

Badri Narayan is a Social Historian and Cultural Anthropologist and currently Director at the G B. Pant Social Science Institute, Prayagraj. His wide ranging interests cover culture, memory and politics, contemporary histories, ethnography of marginalized politics, social and anthropological history, dalit and subaltern issues and Identity formation, Language and the question of power.

He was a recipient of the Fulbright Senior Fellowship (September 2005-April 2006) and the Smuts Fellowship, University of Cambridge (February 2007 – October 2007). He has been a fellow at the Indian Institute of Advanced Study, Shimla (1998-99), Visiting Fellow at the International Institute of Asian Studies, University of Leiden, The Netherlands (2002) and HGIS Fellow at the Royal Tropical Institute, Amsterdam (2001). He has also been Indian Council for Cultural Relations (ICCR) Visiting Professor in The South Asian Studies Programme at the National University of Singapore, Singapore.

Besides having written a number of articles both in English and Hindi, he has authored Kanshiram: Leader of the Dalits, 2014 (Penguin), The Making of the Dalit Public in North India: Uttar Pradesh 1950-present, 2011 (Oxford), Fascinating Hindutva – Saffron Politics and Dalit Mobilisation, 2009 (Sage), Women Heroes and Dalit Assertion in North India, 2006 (Sage), Documenting Dissent, 2001(IIAS Shimla). He has recently edited a volume on languages of Uttar Pradesh- Uttar Pradesh ki Bhashayien, 2016 (Orient Blackswan) by People's Linguistic Survey of India. Due to his academic and literary contribution he has been the recipient of many prestigious literary awards.

Dr. K.N. Bhatt

Dr. K.N. Bhatt is an economist by profession with several years of research experience in development, environment, educational planning and management studies. A Ph.D. from the University of Allahabad, has been working with the Institute since 1984. He has completed a number of research projects relating to education, development and environment decentralization and disaster management. He has authored several research papers, written project reports and published four books.

K. N. Bhatt is a professional researcher in social sciences. He is an environmental economist and has worked on several developmental issues. He has authored, edited and co-edited several books including System of Rice Intensification 2017, Child Labor in India: Empirical Evidence from Glass and Bidi Industries 2015, Agrarian Change and Small Farmers: Super Markets, Viability and Food Policy 2014, Consumers, Consumerism and Consumer Protection: Indian Context 2010, Disaster Risk Management Programme in Uttar Pradesh: Learning from Some Case Studies 2009, Population, Environment and Health: Emerging Concerns 2008, Social Development 2002, Uttarakhand: Ecology, Economy and Society 1997 and has published about four dozen papers in various journals and edited volumes. Dr. K.N. Bhatt is a Professor of Economics at G. B. Pant Social Science Institute, Allahabad Central University, Allahabad.

Email : bhattkn@ gbpssi.org. in, knbhatt1@rediffmail.com